# Things to Consider

### By
### Don Fay

This is Tom's father —
if you read
carefully — you
will recognize
Tom —        Sissy ♡

Things to Consider by Don Fay

Published by Pen It! Publications, LLC

812-371-4128  www.penitpublications.com

Published in the United States of America by Pen It! Publications, LLC

ISBN: 978-1-948390-32-3

# Contents

# Foreword

This is a collection of the pieces I have written over the years. Most have been published, some many times. I've tried to select a diverse representation of the scope of my writing - including a few newspaper writings. Perhaps in the future, I will prepare a volume of them. It is my hope you will enjoy the book and find it profitable reading.

*It seems right that this piece be first, as it was the first one to be published.*

*This work first appeared in <u>Church and Home</u>, April 1955, Standard Pub. Co., 8121 Hamilton Ave, Cincinnati, OH 45231.*

# I WAS AN ORPHAN

I was an orphan when it came time for church. I had to get myself ready and go alone. My friends had their parents there, but I was by myself. I sat with the other kids who, for some reason I couldn't understand, wanted to sit together. How I wished for a mother and a father to sit between! I would have been so proud; I would have sat straight and still. I wouldn't have wiggled an inch. I'd have listened to every word, and when church was over I wouldn't have run with the others but would have walked quietly beside my mom and dad. I would have been so good if I had a mother and father at church. Every day at meal time I had a mother to fix dinner. She washed my clothes and wiped the tears. I had a mother to teach me how to hold my fork and to say *please* and *thank you*. She was there to bandage a cut or care for me when I was sick. I had a mother who worked hard and did a good job of feeding and keeping me clean, but I was an orphan when it came time for church.

I had a father who worked hard to buy the mountains of food and the clothes which wore out so quickly. I had someone to spank me when I was bad, to play, and wrestle with. I had a father who was a pal.

I had two parents who were real great. They understood me and loved me. Their life was their children - to care for, feed, clothe, and house. But I was an orphan when it came time for church!

# Devotionals and Other Readings

*This section of the book is comprised mainly of devotional articles. Some of them are fiction, but if they are so truthful that you can't tell, what difference does it make?*

*First appeared - Today's Christian Mother, Spring 1973, Standard Pub. Co., 8121 Hamilton Ave., Cincinnati, OH 45231.*

# HOW TO REAR CHILDREN

I reached for the battered old book eagerly. I thought it had been lost for good. As I opened it, memories flooded me. The book had been the Bible of my first wife, Mary, given to her by a friend while she was in Bible College. She had it with her the summer we met while doing mission work in New York City. There on the streets of the slums and in the Vacation Bible Schools of the suburban areas, she brought its living words to many who had never known God.

When we were at Bible College together, she always had it with her. In class, she never entered a discussion unless she had something meaningful to say. Then, she would say it quietly and forcefully, reading from her Bible to bear out what she was saying.

After we were married, we moved to Brewerton, NY to serve a small church. The Bible of course, came along. In Bible study she would quietly feed me the facts, or scriptures I needed in a discussion. From its abundant help, she could draw a multitude of obscure facts; with the concordance she could locate just the right scripture.

I enjoyed looking out from the pulpit and seeing her sitting, her Bible open, with the newest baby on her lap. I'll never understand how she was able to keep a young child occupied, and yet follow a sermon so carefully. At times she would become so involved in the sermon that she would forget the baby on her lap, and another page would be torn. The tape that mended them has dried out and is sticking to the other pages now.

When the children were older, I would stop what I was doing and listen as she read to them from the Bible. It seemed so clear and so simple as she read. I realized that she was expressing the difficult passages in simple terms with such fluency that it was hard to tell when she wasn't reading. The stories came alive and became comprehensible to the little ones.

Too many babies on her lap and too much use caused the cover came off. There wasn't money to buy a new one, so she searched through my books for one *just* the right size. She took its cover and put it on her Bible. We laughed about how fitting the title had become – 'How to Rear Children'.

Our youngest was entering school. There was a little extra money then, so we bought a new Bible, with pages of extra helps', but it took Mary awhile to get used to it. Her notes weren't in it, and it didn't open to those favorite passages she knew and loved so much. She continued to use the new Bible, however, and one day the old Bible disappeared. Shortly after her death, at the birth of our sixth child, I found it. It is a rare treasure, reminding me of the fifteen years we were learning from God: 'How to Rear Children'.

# CREATOR

I was so young, yet the images of that day are vivid. Some of the details come from general memories of life on State St. in Batavia, NY. That day, however, affected me so much that I can see it as if it were yesterday.

It was a hot, dead summer day - the day I found a broken bit of antique soft orange brick. The mortar that clung to it sparkled in the blinding sun. It was truly a treasure for a four-year-old to explore.

My world was as dried up as the drought beaten earth. All living creatures sought shelter from the merciless heat - everyone but me. My chubby hand clutched the new-found treasure.

The dog lay panting in the cool dirt under the porch - his tongue hanging out. The cat lay under a tangle of drooping weeds, dozing. Every now and then she opened an eye, only one, to look around.

The street was deserted except for the mystical waves of heat dancing upon the hard surface. The dull green shades at the windows of the sleeping homes were drawn against the sun.

The grass felt cool on my naked knees as I knelt beside the burning sidewalk. My hand held the treasure, a bit of crumbling, ancient orange brick found among the glistening mortar of a long-forgotten foundation. As I reached out and made a tentative swipe on the rough surface of the walk, my breath was caught in the beauty of the sensual orange that splashed across the hard, dead surface.

The lifeless, barren walk soon teemed with newly created existence as my life creating brick swept across the surface. My heart cried out its loneliness on square after square of smooth grey pavement. The vivid, primitive figures I drew lived because I had created them from the dust of my chalk, and had breathed into them my very life. Block after block swarmed with the excitement of newly emerging life. I became intoxicated with my power to reproduce myself, to give my breath to dust.

Then they caught me - face, hands, naked knees so smeared with the life-giving brick that creator and created merged into an almost indistinguishable one. Not only did they reject my cry for love, they meted out punishment with mature innocence and justice. Giving me a bucket of water, and a broom, I was commanded to destroy my masterpiece. I wept as I washed away the life I had created from the dust, from my bit of brick.

Years later, when I heard how God had to wash away His created world in a flood, I wept for Him. I knew a little of how He felt that day when the world was destroyed by a flood. He had an ark, and Noah, and Noah's family, and would be able to create again. But they took away my crumbling brick, my power to create.

# I AM ONLY A MAN

Everyone is asleep: Mary tired from a day of caring for five children; the children tired from the strain of growing so fast. Outside an owl is hooting, perched, probably in a honey locust, watching for a fleeting shadow, a rabbit or a mouse that will satisfy its hunger. It is in these quiet moments that the responsibility of being a father bears down. They sleep, the children and Mary, confident that I can protect and provide for them. Yet, I know that I am but a man, and it is a task far too great for a mere man.

I remember one night - it must have been shortly after I was married. Something awoke me in the night; perhaps it was a noise, or a dream. I don't remember. Whatever it was, it caused me to strain into the darkness. Neither my ears, nor my eyes could pierce the blackness, so I started to drop back into the softness of sleep thinking my father was downstairs, and everything was safe. I was jolted from the creeping haze of sleep. My father wasn't downstairs. Mary, peaceful beside me, was confident of me as I had been of my father. Now, I was the one who was to maintain the peace and security. From that day on, when a board creaked, I was the one upon whom the responsibility rested.

This day comes to every man, and from that day he will hide a gnawing terror knowing his inability; he will hold a false confidence in a strength he does not have, or he will lean upon a father who is there. If he has this faith in God, he will be a successful father. He will not find himself failing his family because of a lack of wisdom, courage, or strength. He will not live in a world of hidden terror, knowing that someday he will need the wisdom, courage, or strength he does not have. He will not suffer the devastating destruction of self-confidence that comes to the man who discovers too late that he is not as wise, as brave or as strong as he always believed himself to be.

The owl has stopped hooting. Perhaps he has found something to eat, or perhaps he has gone elsewhere to look. I'm going to bed now. It is good to be able to sleep knowing that my Father is there should an intruder, or fire, disturb our peace and security. I am only a man, but with a Father like mine, being a man is enough.

# MISS WYNN

Miss Wynn was a terror to all of us who were entering the sixth grade at Brooklyn School in Batavia. A tall, thin woman, her towering height alone was enough to intimidate the gangling pre-teens who faced the ordeal of becoming sixth graders. Her straight black hair was cropped exactly dividing the ear. Her black and grey suits only added to the severity of her appearance. She was *ugly*.

We eased into her room that first day of school, filled with terror, prepared for the worst by last year's sixth graders. The tales they told were too unbelievable to be anything but true. From the start it was obvious that the half hadn't been told. Everyone sank lower in the seat as she explained the rules. Invisibility seemed the best defense. In her class there would be order, proper behavior, and respect - respect for God, country, Miss Wynn, and each other.

The day began with the Lord's Prayer and salute to the flag. It was the Lord's Prayer that terrified me most. I had never learned it. We weren't much for religious things at our home. I did know that the Catholic version ended before the Protestant, and Miss Wynn was a Catholic. I had visions of her coming to the Catholic end and leaving me to find my own way to the end as a Protestant. The Catholic kids quit when they were supposed to, and she continued with us all the way to the end. Perhaps things wouldn't be as bad as it seemed.

Students were seated alphabetically, and when papers were handed in those in the back passed their paper over their right shoulder to the person ahead of them. That student placed his on top and passed it over the right shoulder of the person ahead of him. So, it continued until all the papers were at the front seats. The student at the front seat to the right stood and collected all the papers, placing each pile on top until all the papers were collected in exact order. Woe to the student who passed over the left shoulder or who put his on the bottom.

Instructions were to be followed explicitly. "I need them in order because when I correct them I like to be able to see in my mind the student whose paper I'm correcting," Miss Wynn explained. She had a reasonable purpose behind every rule.

When reciting, we stood beside our seat, both feet on the floor and responded, "Yes Miss Wynn," or "No, Miss Wynn." When we were done we were expected to say, "Thank you," before we sat down. Such things were already out of date which is why Miss Wynn taught at Brooklyn School. We were to get the worst of everything at that school. Washington School in the better part of town, got the best.

Though it was a terrifying experience to enter sixth grade at Brooklyn School, we soon loved it, loved Miss Wynn, and saw her as a beautiful woman. For many of us, it was the first time we had order in our lives. We always knew what to expect: fairness, order, respect, and the challenge to be what she knew we were destined to become.

When she took us outside to play, she would occasionally umpire a ball game. Usually, she allowed us to organize our own games. Aware of the hurt felt by the last chosen for a game, she explained that we would have more time to play if we kept the same teams each day. No more standing, waiting, fearing to be the last chosen. If the winning team was too exuberant, once inside we received the lecture on learning to lose well and win graciously.

Once, when I had excelled (a rare thing for me) she took my bragging for a short time. She then put a stop to it with some of the most important words I have ever learned. "You can always find some not as well as you. Don't brag until you can find no one better."

It was Miss Wynn who taught me to love books. She seemed to know when we were tired and would read to us. It was in her class that I was introduced to John Steinbeck's, *The Red Pony*. When she got to the part about the mare being taken to the stud, she skipped hurriedly over it. Years later, while reading it, I discovered the graphic parts she had left out.

I'll never forget the day she caught one of her favorites cheating at math. She snapped her math book shut, the explosive sound bringing all the startled class to attention. "It isn't important whether I teach you to read, or spell, or multiply; if you go out of my class and don't know how to live, I've failed." She spent the rest of math class teaching us the value of honesty.

It was this that made Miss Wynn an exceptional teacher. For five years we had been in school without a qualified teacher. The first-grade teacher specialized in destroying any love of learning we might have had. The second-grade teacher had been an expert at destroying creativity. The third-grade teacher taught boredom, and the fourth-grade teacher had endless anecdotes about her niece. In fifth-grade we were taught but that was all; any learning was accidental. With Miss Wynn, we were prepared for life. It was as if she was aware of the years of neglect we had suffered; we were determined to make it up, to reawaken the love for books, learning, order, discipline, and morality.

We left with a respect for God, our country, our teacher and most of all, for our self.

What a shame that she would not be allowed to teach today.

*Published in Joyful Woman 3-17-92, Live Nov. 2013*

*This is a true story written from my daughter's view point.*

# BETH'S BEAUTIFUL BIRTHDAY

By: Jerita Fay Maynard

**I**t's going to be awful - just awful!" y youngest sister, Beth, cried. "Dad tries hard, but can you see him making a cake?"

I was setting the table. The plates and silver clattered so loudly that I suddenly realized I was expressing my own hurt. I took a deep breath, gently set the next plate, and carefully turned it so the design was straight - like my mother would have done. Five places for the kids, one for Dad, and one for Grandma. The baby wasn't big enough to come to the table.

"Dad can make a good cake," I said, but I remembered the hem he had put in Marisa's new dress and how it came out during church. I was so embarrassed.

"His cake won't taste like Mom's," Beth sobbed. Tears began to run down her plump cheeks. Being the youngest, except for the new baby, she got away with tears. I wondered if they would work as well now that we had a new brother.

"She made Joel a train cake with gum drops and cherries," Beth continued. "Lesana has a lamb, a white one with coconut and fluffy white frosting that stuck to my nose. You had a beautiful girl with a full white dress trimmed in real violets coated with sugar. If I get anything, it will be a lopsided, lumpy cake with gooey frosting. Why did Mom have to die before my birthday? She loved God so. Why did He let her die?"

Beth's tears flowed again, and I looked away. I was the oldest and was needed. Fourteen is too young to always be needed. I wanted out.

"I'm sure Mom had a special one planned for me, and it died with her. I'll never see it," Beth wailed.

I searched the faith I had learned from my mother to find a scrap of remaining hope to share. There was nothing left. I had used it up. I had *so* depended upon her to strengthen my faith.

"Maybe he made you a cake last night," was the best I could do.

"No, I've looked everywhere," Beth said quietly. "Joel even helped me look. There isn't a cake". Then the tears, silent this time, again rolled over her cheeks.

That's what made it frustrating. There wasn't anyone to blame. Dad tried to make it work. He really did. He just couldn't fill Mom's place. There was this big, empty spot. Mom had been an important part of every moment. It wasn't anyone's fault. I knew I had to accept it, but I didn't know how to help Beth.

Dad came home from work without a cake. Beth's last hope was gone. A store bought cake would have been better than nothing. She didn't say anything – she didn't even cry.

I shared her hurt but didn't want to. I had too much of my own. I could have taken the tears, but her resignation was too much. There was no place to escape. Supper had to be put on the table.

It was hash again for supper. Grandma always made hash out of the leftover tough, cheap roasts Dad could afford to buy. It wasn't Beth's favorite, or mine. Mom let us choose whatever we wanted for our birthday supper. Even in the hardest of times there was something special.

Tonight, there was no decoration, nothing different from every other meal. I should have done something. I could have tried. Somewhere there were colored streamers.

The limp curtains hung at the dirty windows. The plastic tablecloth was torn. Three of the plates were now chipped. Suddenly I saw how changed everything really was. Again, the anger surged, not at my mother for dying, not at my dad who was trying, not even at Grandma who just didn't understand.

My mother would have said that God always knows what He is doing. My dad said that Mom deserved the rest. It was up to us to trust God to see us through to the special times that were ahead. I needed something more.

"Can we give her our gifts?" Joel asked trying to dispel the gloom.

"Not until we light the cake," my father said.

"Cake? There isn't a cake. Joel and I looked everywhere," Beth said, her eyes widening with the rekindled hope.

Suddenly dinner was forgotten, and an almost forgotten joy returned.

My father pushed his half-eaten supper away. Slowly, wearily he got to his feet. The cake wouldn't wait.

"Did you think to look in the freezer?" he asked.

He left the kitchen and returned in a few minutes with a huge mound of frozen white goo. Candles spurted at rakish angles. M&M's slowly slipped down the sides. A barely discernible haze rose from the cold surface. It was a laudable concoction of everything sweet and good thrown together in hopeful confusion.

"It's beautiful," Beth gasped. "When did you make it?"

"Last night," Dad replied as he cut down through the whipped topping that covered alternating layers of store bought angel food cake and ice cream.

I remembered hearing him come to bed late. I had been too sleepy to wonder why.

Suddenly, the cake became the most beautiful cake in the entire world. I knew we would survive without our mother. It wouldn't be easy, but we'd find those special times that were ahead. Dad, with the wisdom and strength God was giving him, would be able to help us through. He would not fail because God would not fail him.

Today, when times are tough, when we reach the limit of our faith, someone makes an ice cream cake, but never quite like the one Dad made.

# MORE REST ROOMS

*The editor turned this one down. He thanked me for the laugh he had.*

Dan Schantz's humorous article on the state of rest rooms in some churches (Christian Standard, "Reflections", Nov. 28, 1993) missed a couple of the worse.

My first wife, Mary, used to get five children ready every Sunday for church. We drove one hundred miles to the Tulley church, which was lost among the mountains south of Syracuse, NY. The once proud church had been started by Alexander Campbell. In its day, the building had been most impressive. To my children it was spectacular. It had the only two story outhouse they had ever seen.

Actually, it might not fit the classification of outhouse. It was fastened to the back of the building. The second story unit of the out house was built over and out beyond the one on the first floor. A shoot like box dropped from the second floor down behind the first floor privy.

We never had to make a potty stop on the way to church. The children held everything in and then made a mad dash upon our arrival. Some headed for the upstairs, which they considered the superior experience. Others headed for the first floor where they could hear everything that came cascading down.

Six years ago, I accepted a call to the Cogan House Christian Church. This is a small church hidden back in the mountains of Pennsylvania. It has the 'necessary Building' out back.

Before I came, the congregation heroically attempted to make the "Necessary Building" unnecessary. Propane toilets were installed. When a person got up from the seat, propane heaters were expected to incinerate all the waste.

They got out of sequence. One Sunday morning before church a lady sat down. They turned on. She came boiling out. It is said she had roast rump.

One day, I wondered what had gotten into a pre-teen boy. He was in front of the 'necessary building' dancing around with his pants down. The wasps, which always built nests in the outhouse, had gotten into his pants.

My present wife, Betsy, who played the piano, was late one morning. It was time to start, and she was nowhere to be seen. Suddenly, she appeared all out of breath. As she rushed past on her way to the piano, she said, "I got locked in the outhouse." Like most out houses, the one at Cogan House had a bit of wood with a screw in the middle to hold the door closed when it wasn't in use. It had turned, locking Betsy in. A woman, arriving late for church, set her free.

After three years of struggling with the DER and Labor and Industry, this small congregation finally left the nineteenth century, and entered the twentieth. It was nip and tuck whether they would make it before the twenty-first arrived.

On a cold Sunday just before Christmas (the temperature had dipped to seventeen below that morning), the congregation rejoiced and gave thanks to the Lord over the toilets that flushed. It was heartfelt joy.

One woman, inspecting the new ladies rest room, remarked that it was big enough to use for a class room. Who knows? The church just might grow so fast it will have to double as one. Growing churches have large, modern, clean, rest rooms. It just might be time to redo yours.

*Portions of this article first appeared as an editorial in the Williamsport, PA, Sun-Gazette July 24, 1993*

# WHEN LIFE IS TOUGH

It seems as if yesterday, but really was a number of years ago – that time I sat alone in the emptiness of a night without end. The institutional green of the room closed over me like a suffocating mist. The steel doors down the hall stood guard against me. Behind them lay Mary struggling to give birth to our sixth child. I sank, helpless, into the institutional chair that gave no comfort, nor was there anyone to comfort me.

Weariness overwhelmed me, then sleep - deep, total sleep.

A cry from Mary awakened me. Confused- Where was I? Had I really heard her call echo down the empty hall? "Don-n-n" still rang in my ears.

The steel doors remained closed - impenetrable. My ears strained, probing the empty silence of the room, seeking to again hear the call.

The weariness was gone as suddenly as it had come.

A low rumble thundered down the hall. Two technicians pushed a cart through the double doors which promptly closed, shutting me out again - an endless, lonely wait.

The doors clanged open, and I started from my chair to greet Mary and the baby; that's how it was supposed to be. Instead, a very young, very scared nurse came through with only a baby.

"Where's Mary?" I asked. "How is she?"

"It's a boy," she said, trying to control the terror in her voice.

Holding him out to me, she tried to draw my attention to the child. I would not be distracted. "The doctor will be out in a moment," she said fleeing with the child, whom I really hadn't seen.

She was no sooner gone when I started to feel guilty that I had not made it easier for her - sorry I had not taken my son into my arms.

I waited, forever in an empty room, in an existence without time.

Then the doctor came out and time began again.

"I know," I said.

"Would you like to see her?" he asked.

I nodded.

Mary's not here, I thought as I looked at the very pale body on the table. She called to me as she passed.

"What will you do now?" the doctor asked.

"*What would I do,*" the doctor asked, more to fill the silence than to seek information.

What would I do? What was there to do? I would go home and tell each of our five children they had a new baby brother. Then, before their joy became too great, I would tell them their mother died.

Romans 8 is sometimes very hard to accept.

Romans 8:28 "And we know that in all things God works for the good of those who love him… 31 What, then shall we say in response to this? If God is for us, who can be against us? 32 He who did not spare his own Son, but gave him up for all – how will he not also, along with him, graciously give us all things?"

Romans 8:35 "Who shall separate us from the love of Christ? Shall trouble or hardship or persecution or famine or nakedness or danger or sword?"

Romans 8:37 "No, in all these things we are more than conquerors through him who loved us. 38 For I am convinced that neither death nor life… 39 neither height nor depth, nor anything else in all creation, will be able to separate us from the love of God that in Christ our Lord."

These verses not only promise us the enabling presence of the Lord, they promise times when faith will be tried - times when nothing less than faith will be enough. When these times hit us, it is how we respond, not the tragedy we suffer, that determines the kind of person we become because of them. When we are overwhelmed in sorrow or fear, in hurt or weariness, it is *we* who decide whether we will be swept away or grasp the hand that reaches down from heaven. The hand is always there for God's children.

We decide whether we will respond in bitterness and anger, or in forgiveness and love. In our choice we determine whether we will be changed into a more understanding, more helpful person, or if we will slowly shrivel into the worthless nothingness of a life filled with self-pity.

In that long wait for the doctor to come out from the steel doors, a friend, a nurse, meaning well, told me the blood they had rushed to my dying wife was out of date. They couldn't use it to save her life.

"You can't afford bitterness." I did not hear the words. I just knew them in that moment when anger and bitterness began to form.

As I stepped from the hospital into the pre-dawn August morning, the air was warm and still. It was as if God had wrapped His arms around me and was holding me in the warmth of His love. There was just enough pre-dawn light that it did not seem dark.

On the short drive home, I heard a truth. It was not like a voice speaking. It was there already in my head. "Take each day as it comes, and my grace will be sufficient to see you through. Each day has enough trouble. Don't borrow tomorrow's."

His grace was sufficient for each day. Late each evening I had just enough energy to crawl into bed. Each morning I awoke, weary, as if I had not slept. Yet the day passed, His hand in mine, until we passed together through that long dark valley into the warm, gentle sun of a new day.

# SUPER MOM

*This article won first place at St. David Christian Writer's Clinic. No one has bought it.*

At the crack of dawn, she jumps from her bed, enters the phone booth hidden in her closet, and changes into her SUPER MOM costume. Flying down the stairs, she starts the coffee. In a single bound she is back up the stairs, pulls her husband from the bed, and props him in the shower.

Faster than a speeding bullet, she enters each child's room, gently awakens the child, collects the dirty clothes and leaves clean clothes neatly laid out.

She again flies down the stairs, begins to prepare a well-balanced breakfast - no sugar, low cholesterol, high complex carbohydrates.

With super speed, she puts a load of clothes in the washer, folds the clean ones in the dryer, and shoots back up the stairs taking them four at a time. She stands her husband in front of the mirror, chases the kids downstairs, gives the baby a bath and dresses him.

She flies downstairs, feeds the kids the breakfast they hate (coaxing them to eat the nourishing food) and packs perfect lunches (preparing fresh carrot sticks and polishing the apples to make them more appetizing).

Using her telescopic vision, she begins the search for her husband's brief case. At the same time, she signs permission slips for field trips, after school events, Girl Scouts, Cub Scouts, early release for a visit to the dentist, and one for her husband to have lunch with the office staff.

Her computer-like mind quickly formulates an elaborate plan for getting everyone to where they need to be after school. It then computes the same for picking them up afterward.

She locates her husband's briefcase and pushes him out the door with a quick kiss just as his ride appears. Finding her kids' books and checking to make sure they have their homework, she signs excuses, gives out milk money, money for tickets for coming events, money for Girl Scouts, Cub Scouts, and pushes them out the door toward the honking large yellow beast, which promptly swallows them through a hole in its side. She releases a sigh of relief as they disappear from sight.

Without a moment to lose, she washes oatmeal from the face, hands, and hair of the baby, puts him squalling into the play pen, and rushes up the stairs two at a time. She dashes into the phone booth and strips off the SUPER MOM costume. After a quick shower, she changes into her disguise, a business suit, grabs the baby under one arm, her brief case and diaper bag in the other, and spurts to the babysitter's.

She arrives at work smart and snappy, ready to begin a day of competitively climbing the corporate ladder in a man's world.

Leaving work at a full gallop, she collects the baby from the sitter, picks up the oldest from high school, drops her at piano lessons, wings off to the elementary school to pick up one for Little League, another for Girl Scouts, sweeps to the dry cleaners, and then scorches the road to the grocery store.

Using her x-ray vision to check the quality of the food, she rapidly computes the cost and value of each item. With one hand, she fills the cart while with the other she replaces the items the baby has pulled from the shelf. With supersonic speed, she heads for home where her super human strength enables her to get the baby and bulging sacks of groceries from the car to the house. Momentarily entering the phone booth and donning her SUPER MOM costume, she puts away all the groceries and starts dinner.

Reverting to her disguise as suburban mom, she again grabs the baby and begins the hectic trip to pick up all the children on time. She helps them with their homework while putting their supper on the table. While they are eating, as quick-as-lightning, she dons the disguise of alluring wife of successful business man. Then, she zips to pick up the baby sitter.

On the double, she gets the children ready for bed, hears their prayers, answers their profound questions, and leaves with her husband for a business dinner. She pushes to make it to the dinner party given by her boss.

After driving the baby sitter home, she stumbles into bed where she struggles to enjoy a moment of urgent love-making before falling exhaustingly into a troubled sleep.

There are all too many Super Moms today. While trying to balance the life of wife and mother with their career, they make themselves vulnerable for total burnout.

Super Mom is not a super mom. Whether she has a career, or spends her time in community projects, excessive activity leaves her unfulfilled. The result is an unfortunate woman who is driven by the unreasonable expectations she takes upon herself.

It is time to face reality. Doing for her family what they ought to be doing for themselves, destroys them. Getting a sense of worth by dominating the family and making them dependent won't meet her needs. Giving the kind of love that requires each member of the family to carry a reasonable share of the responsibility, however, will.

Get with *it*, Super Mom. The praise of those around you is hollow. You don't have everyone fooled. Real joy and admiration will come when you let go of those you love. Give them a chance to stand on their own feet; expect them to carry a reasonable share of the load, *then* their love will be sincere and satisfying and your joy complete.

*First appeared in Light and Life, Jan. 1988.*

# SPECIAL GIFT

Prayer at dinner is a good time to remember God's loving kindness. I've tried many ways to make it a season of praising the goodness of God, but prayers at our table have a way of becoming unacceptably repetitive.

Once, after my son said the prayer, I asked him if that was the best God had given to him. "That's all I can think of," Jonathan replied. We talked about his day and found he remembered little for which to be grateful.

I tried warning him ahead that he would be called on and to think about what the Lord had done for us. His prayers didn't improve much.

One day after I warned him that it was his turn to pray, Jonathan came to the table with a long list and a twinkle in his eye. I quickly reminded him that the Lord doesn't appreciate long prayers, but he won his point.

Even setting the example and expressing deep gratitude that my children were such a joy to me it didn't work. Somehow, no matter what we did, we usually reverted to the same well-worn phrases that reflect a lack of awareness of God's great goodness. My wife had her usual opening phrase, I had my standard gratitude, and the children rushed through their mini prayers.

What is the use of praying before we eat if we aren't going to think about what we are saying, and don't have gratitude in our hearts?

A minister told me about a most unusual woman in a church he served. She was the wealthiest member of the congregation and was able to afford any material things she might desire. She sought after the gifts that God freely gives.

Upon awakening, she asked herself what special gift God would give her that day. All day she watched, expectant, confident there would be a unique gift from God.

She found it in the first soft violet of spring, a bright Cardinal on a drab winter bush, a child's warming smile of acceptance. God never failed her and she never had to rely on her wealth for her joy. Because of this, her life was filled with hope and rich blessings beyond measure.

In this story I found the answer to our need for meaningful prayer at the dinner table. I changed from my usual practice of calling on a single member of the family to give thanks to the Lord. Instead we all prayed, each of us in turn, thanking God for the finest gift we had received that day. I encouraged them to forget the traditional prayer form and to simply thank God for that day's gift of joy.

We are slowly learning the skill of gratitude. We are also learning to awake each morning looking for a rare blessing from God. Even more important is the result of sharing of our happiness with the others at the supper table. Most of all, we are becoming aware of the grace and mercy of God that once passed unnoticed.

Hopefully, we also will learn to find our joy in life from the special gifts of God. This is a joy that no one will be able to take from us. It will become a wealth that will not be lost to fire or storm, rust, moth, or thief.

# ALL HER OWN TEETH

Her immense, shapeless bulk seemed to fill the huge throne-like chair. Her head and shoulder protruded above the mass of sagging flesh giving it only a semblance of shape. I shifted my weight from one foot to the other as she left my father and me standing in her august presence.

The feeble light from the small lamp next to chair was swallowed up by the high ceilings and old heavy drapes. The huge silver service, which burdened a frail table with its load, seemed to lurk in the dark shadows of the immense room as if afraid to expose itself.

The corner of my eye caught a glimpse of my father. He cowed off to one side, a silly apologetic grin on a worn thin face. His head was slightly bowed, shoulders dropped. The old, worn, sweat stained hat was tightly grasped in his clenched fist.

A growing hatred for this woman welled up in me as she droned on about how faithfully my father had once served her. While a teen, he braved the winter cold to stoke her furnace before school. She told how he would stop by after school to carry out the ashes and how he continued to serve her faithfully even after he had a family.

She spoke to him as if he were still a kid and as if he were still dependent upon her for the pittance with which she had once rewarded his faithfulness. He slunk even further into the shadows at the sound of her raspy voice. I resented her power that seemed to make him insignificant in her presence.

She told me of her family - of their importance and respectability as early residents of the small city.

I raised my eyes a little and mumbled, "Mine came over in 1642. They were French Huguenots, all of whom were killed during the persecution, except for the ones who escaped to Wales."

She cleared her throat noisily, as if impatient with my impudence, and I saw my father shift uneasily. He lifted his tired shoulders a bit and his smile changed from nervous timidity to joy in seeing this tyrant challenged.

She didn't seem to notice the change in him, believing him capable of nothing more than the humility with which he had served her.

She continued her self-praise telling how by hard work and thrift she and her husband had been able to, "save the little we have and send our son and grandsons to Harvard."

My nose began to itch, and my head ached from the terrible stench that seemed to hang about her in the stale air.

*I wonder if she knows how badly she stinks,* I thought, and then looked desperately for some place to hide the giggle that was running up and down my spine. As the giggle eased away, I realized what a ridiculous person she really was, what a worthless and meaningless life she had lived. The terror I felt when I first stood in her intimidating presence, left. I straightened up, squaring my young shoulders, lifting my head a little, yet keeping it bowed enough to mask my growing arrogance. I spread my feet apart and rested my weight firmly on them both, and stood proud of my family, my father. Their life had counted for something good, though poor, as they.

She was very perceptive in spite of her age, and noting the change in my bearing, stumbled over the words as she hurried on to tell me that she had never sinned. She snapped the words proudly with finality that caused my father to cringe before this formidable force of self-proclaimed nobility and piety. Rather than being intimidated by this terrible revelation, I found myself praying silently, "Oh Lord, save me from sinlessness. I'd hate to end up like her."

Realizing that I had not been brought to heel, had not been humbled by her holy presence, she tried again, this time with an even greater revelation.

"I'm over eighty years old and still have all of my own teeth," she boasted as she smiled an artificial grin to display them. I peered intently through the gloom to see if she was lying about this also. Even in the poor light I could see they were original equipment, even though they were discolored and worn.

I thought, *"I'm still in high school and my teeth are rotting because there is no milk, no tooth brush, or tooth powder, and no money for a dentist because you and your kind were thrifty and saved what you had, giving as little as possible to those whose faithful service you so treasured."*

She continued to pound me with words, trying to bend me into the subjection she expected of those who worked for her. I stood tall, polite, but unmoved, secure in the knowledge of who I was.

"Your *father* was a good worker," she said giving the word such emphasis as if to suggest that I would not be his equal.

"I hope you will be as good."

"My father has taught me well. It is part of the legacy he has left me." My words restored my father's confidence, the confidence I had seen drain from him the moment we had entered this evil presence. I felt his soft love reach out to me, discernible, in spite of the hot, close, oppressiveness of the room. He strengthened me.

"I expect honesty and integrity from the people who work for me. Can I trust you?"

The question angered me not only because of its implication, but because it *again* made my father seem small and insignificant in her presence.

"My father is one of the most trusted and respected men in this community. Respect is the only thing this town has ever given him. I would never do anything to take that from him." The firmness in my voice unsettled her.

"Very well," she said with a sharpness that expressed her anger. "I will pay you fifty cents an hour. I expect you to be here right after school every Wednesday to mow my lawn. You are to pick up all the sticks before you mow and sweep the walks when you are finished."

I felt a bit uneasy about what I knew I had to say. There was no way around it. Perhaps I'd be pushing my luck. This old tiger might still have teeth.

"I'm a Fay. People appreciate the quality of my work. They pay me two-fifty an hour. I can't afford to work for less than that. If that is more than you can afford, I'll find a friend to do it for you," I said with a quietness that was properly respectful.

I heard my dad suck in his breath. She glared at me for a moment. She knew I had her in a bind.

"Very well, I will pay that, but only for work as good as your father did," she said trying desperately to minimize her defeat.

As we left, my father rested his rough hand lightly on my shoulder. Neither of us spoke, but I understood what he was saying.

*First appeared Seek, Dec. 22, 1991*

# GIFT OF GOLD

The huge doors wouldn't budge. I stretched again to reach the heavy brass knob. My courage, barely enough to bring me up the steps, was now drained by the stubborn door.

Why, when nobody asked me to come, was I trying so hard to get to Sunday school? I pushed again, but the doors didn't budge so I turned away, relieved of the terror of facing a new experience. Just as I was about to flee down the steps, a man pushed them open a crack and peered out.

"I thought I heard someone at the door. Come in. I didn't expect to see such a little girl," he said with such warmth that I began to feel better about coming.

He showed me to a room where other third graders had already begun class. I tried to slip unnoticed into an empty chair. Everyone was so clean, so well dressed. They peeked at me out of the corner of their eyes with obvious curiosity. The lady who was reading, looked up.

A smile came quickly to her face. It seemed to reach across the room, and touch me gently. I no longer felt the need to become invisible, to slip out of sight beneath the table. When she said, "Welcome, I'm so glad you came," the words made me feel sort of warm. Having never been loved I didn't know what the glow was, just knew it was the something unknown I was seeking. Quite unexpectedly, when all hope of ever discovering it was gone, there it was.

From the start, the lady made me feel special. It was the way she always called me Violet, which made me feel beautiful. She never called me Vi as my mother did. The nickname made me feel cheap, worthless.

I began to look forward to the Sunday morning moment of belonging, of being loved. It was the only beautiful moment in my week.

On my second Sunday, a very pretty girl in a very frilly dress jumped up as soon as I came in. She took my hand and asked me to sit with her.

For once, my rumpled clothes - dirt and all, didn't seem to matter.

I didn't realize it, but they were teaching me to love. I was learning about the Jesus everyone seemed to know. I was beginning to love. The change came slowly as I began to understand that He was the spring from which this new-found love flowed. I longed for some way to tell Him how happy I had become. When the chance came, I couldn't take part.

The church had set aside a day to bring a gift of love to Jesus, and I had nothing to bring. I spent all week looking for something. The corner of the dirty room where I slept on a bare mattress was void of anything beautiful. My life, except for the lovely moment Sunday morning, was empty. Among the few things I owned, there was nothing good enough to give.

That night I couldn't sleep. The smells and noise of the bar down below kept awakening me. The old coat I used as a blanket kept slipping off. My legs ached from the cold. I cried quietly knowing from experience that if mother (working down stairs) heard, I would get a beating. It had always been that way for as long as I could remember.

I awoke to a bright morning sun that only made me more despondent by its joyful exuberance. Washing as best I could in the small basin of cold water, the chill of fall, and the tingling of the cold water left my whole body shaking. The worn dress I had tried to wash out the night before was still badly stained, wrinkled, and a bit damp. My tangled, greasy hair just wouldn't brush out.

Fighting back the tear and knowing I would have no gift to bring, I ate the cold bit of pizza my mother had brought home from her night of partying. Still hungry, I looked about hoping for something else to eat. There was nothing. Head drooping, feet dragging, I started for the church pulling the coat together against the cold as best I could.

It wouldn't matter to them that I had no gift. Jesus would understand. I knew that was so, but it did matter to *me*.

When I reached the corner where I turned toward the church building and away from the rot and filth of my neighborhood, I looked across the empty lot. There among the rotting mattresses, rusting cans, and broken bottles, a simple flower had managed to miraculously survive.

It was so beautiful that I gasped for breath. The deep yellow petals surrounding the soft, dark brown center warmed my chilled body. If only I could share this great joy that I suddenly felt with my friends who loved me. Digging in the trash I found a dirty, dark blue bottle. In an old pan filled with rusty rain water, I scrubbed away the dirt, filled the bottle with water and picked the flower.

It had taken too much time. I hurried, no longer wanting to be late so as to not miss the giving of the gifts.

The last of the gifts were being carried forward as I arrived. The front of the church was piled high with food for the poor, money to help the needy, and clothing. Someone had given a beautiful dress that looked to be my size. Beside it was a warm coat.

The gifts were so beautiful, and so thoughtful. The flowers in the old blue bottle suddenly seemed so poor, so plain, so unworthy. I started to turn away, ashamed of my gift when my Sunday school teacher saw me.

"Look what Violet brought!" she cried with excitement.

Everyone turned to look. I had no choice but to walk all the way to the front carrying the Black-Eyed Susan. Someone moved aside the beautiful love given gifts to make room for mine.

As I placed it on the altar, the sun burst through the window and transformed the flowers into shining gold. People gasped at the sudden beauty, and I cried with joy, knowing that the flowers had brought to others the same joy they had given to me.

*Published in Seek 3/18/2001.*

# BAG LADY

I did not expect to encounter the bag lady the day three of my seven children and I left the City Underground in Toronto. Nor did I expect the encounter to affect me so profoundly.

It had been an exciting evening of wandering through stores filled with dreams we couldn't afford. We had gone to the upper level that rose above the subterranean stores and were descending a huge stairway to the outside.

On one of the steps squatted an old bag lady. Her rank smell reached us long before we got to her. She sat protecting her bags of precious belongings which were clustered about her. In a few hours she would be forced out into the Canadian cold.

As we passed by, she looked up and bombarded me with filthy, abusive words. The attack was unprovoked and so unexpected that I was caught off guard. My response was to rush my children away to safety as fast as I could.

It was not easy to answer their questions about the woman. I was smarting from the assault and found it hard to feel compassionate toward her. It was even more difficult envisioning Christ loving her enough to die for her. I did not want to be concerned for, much less love, this repulsive person.

Technically, as a Christian, I believed there were workable Biblical solutions to the problem of homelessness (the homeless being an abstraction of anonymous people, living somewhere else). It was upsetting to realize that God was asking me to care about this vile person. I would have preferred my close encounter with homelessness to be a single mother with three delightful children. That I could have handled.

From that day it was no longer possible for me to think of the homeless as featureless people: the image of this filthy woman of the gutters would not leave me.

Most of all, the encounter taught me I was not the Christian I though myself to be. It left me searching for the grace to love the unlovable. Now, when I read Matt. 5:43-48 I am reminded how far I am from what the Lord expects me to become.

How is it possible to love the unlovable? I try. Sometimes I succeed - a little. It is a struggle. My goal is to succeed often. If God had made them more loveable it wouldn't be so hard. But that is the whole point. God challenges us to let His grace change us into loving people.

"You have heard that it was said, 'Love your neighbor and hate your enemy.' [44] But I tell you: Love your enemies and pray for those who persecute you, [45] that you may be sons of your Father in heaven. He causes his sun to rise on the evil and the good and sends rain on the righteous and the unrighteous. [46] If you love those who love you, what reward will you get? Are not even the tax collectors doing that? [47] And if you greet only your brothers, what are you doing more than others? Do not even pagans do that? [48] Be perfect, therefore, as your heavenly Father is perfect".

*The New International Version, (Grand Rapids, MI: Zondervan Publishing House) 1984.*

*Appeared Neighborhood Christian 2-19-1956,
Lutheran Digest 10-29-89, Together 11-7-94*

# PRAYER OF A BRAVE MAN

I've asked you to give me a lot of things, Lord. You've been most gracious, giving me rich gifts. Now I want You to take some of them back. I hope You will not think me ungrateful. You see, I've misused them, and they have turned from blessings to great hindrances.

I've become full of overpowering, blinding pride because of all the ability you gave me. I thought it would enable me to do great things for You. Instead it is a hindrance. Because of my pride, all that ability keeps getting in the way of serving You.

When I accomplish a difficult task and do an exceptional job, I forget it was Your gifts that enabled me. I believe I can do great things all by myself. Forgetting that it is You who are behind what I do, I lose my effectiveness.

So, I find I need to ask You to take away my talent and ability and with it take this blinding pride. Perhaps then I will remember that it is You working in me.

We are never hungry. My table is always filled with abundance. My freezer is full. We eat well.

I keep thinking I have provided all this for my family forgetting that all good gifts come from You. When I thank You before the meal, I seldom mean it.

Take it from me. Make me ask for my daily bread. Then perhaps I will again feast on Your Word and eat my bread with true thanksgiving.

My clothes though abundant and good, sometimes I wish I could afford the new and expensive styles, but those I have are warm and most comfortable. I have more than I need. Before they are worn out they are replaced with new. I am proud of the way people notice me when I am dressed.

I know better. You have made it very clear that the only suitable clothing is the righteousness

You provide. Could You take away these vain coverings and replace them with a blood washed robe?

I live in a land of freedom and security. I am protected and there is little cause for worry.

I love being free. It is a gift many do not enjoy. You can see what this freedom and security has been doing to me.

It keeps me from learning to trust in Your loving protection. I trust in my nation. I expect it to keep me secure.

It can't protect me from the always eventual death. I am not ready to die because I have not learned of Your power to keep me secure through all danger.

I need a faith greater than I can learn when I am so protected from harm. Take this freedom and security from me that I might learn to trust in You. Your gift is good, but I am not strong enough to enjoy it.

I have a warm, beautiful home. It is such a joy I sometimes wishes I could spend eternity in it. I love it so much that I spend too much of my time and strength maintaining it. I no longer long for the far greater home You have promised.

Take even this from me. Take it gently as possible because it has become a part of me. Take it, but at the same time give me the promise and vision of a much better place. Renew my faith in the eternal, perfect home You have gone to prepare for me.

My sight, my health, and my intellect You meant for my good. They've become a hindrance because of the way I have abused them. If they must be taken before I can see You as truth, stand in Your strength, or know Your salvation, then take them.

Those I love I do not want to give up. Help me to so love others that my love for You will be real.

Thank You, Lord. I am sure things will get better now. I am sorry that I abused Your good gifts. I know I will be better without them.

# THE LORD'S MAN

*This is a work of fiction. What it says about those who serve the Lord is true.*

I travel a lot on my job and often am gone over the weekend. That is how I happened to find the little congregation lost in the hills of Kentucky. Rather than attend the large city church, I drove to a country town and found a small, neglected building. It was the strange contrast that made me stop. Everything about the building spoke of neglect and unconcern except little things, delicate flowers growing along the walk, the lawn carefully cut, ingenious attempts to repair the neglected building.

An old man greeted me with a warm welcome that told me I had made a good choice. The others there were busy about their own affairs, many coming late. The preacher was young. His sermon was well prepared and well delivered, but he obviously was troubled.

The old man and his wife invited me to dinner and I accepted, the simple meal was the best I had eaten in a long time. They didn't say much about the problems of the church, but it slowly came out. "Since you're a traveling man, and get around and meet a lot of people, perhaps you can help me," he asked. "I've got to find us a new preacher."

"It is hard for small congregations to hold young men," I said. "Your preacher preaches a good sermon and seems to be exceptional. It's shame some of these young men aren't willing to stay with the small congregations."

"He's willing to stay. The people don't want him. He is the seventh in five years." There was a trace of bitterness in the old lady's voice.

"This time I get to do the choosing. I said I wouldn't find a new preacher unless they would give me the right to hire him for a year. They also agreed to increase the pay to Seventy Dollars plus the old parsonage. They won't pay utilities. It costs too much to heat the place" The old man spoke excitedly about the arrangements. He had always had to find the candidates for the pulpit, but this was the first time he would get to do the selecting.

"What kind of a man would they like?" I asked.

"What they want is someone about thirty, with the experience of a man of eighty, the strength and enthusiasm of a lad of twenty, and the intelligence of a college professor. They want him to look like a Greek god, have the tact of a politician, and be as submissive as a two-year old. But they aren't going to get what they want." There was a twinkle in the old man's eyes. "I'm looking for the man the Lord wants us to have. I doubt if he'll be any of the things they think they want. That doesn't matter. Somewhere the Lord has just the man for us. He's the man I'm looking for and I'll know him when I see him."

I took the old man's name and address, intending to try to help in return for his hospitality. I met several young preachers and suggested they apply but they had heard about the congregation. They wouldn't go for any wage.

Then one day I met a man who was about as close to nothing as you can get. He just didn't have it. He spent ten years trying to get through Bible College. He really tried. They finally asked him to leave. It was the only time the college had found someone so hopeless that they gave up. He not only stuttered, but also he just couldn't put words together so they made sense. I didn't see how he could possibly make himself understood. He wasn't blind but his eyes were so bad that he couldn't drive a car. He knew how to read but he had to study the words out and it was a slow process for him. He had a most amazing ability to say things in the worst possible way. I couldn't possibly tell how old he was. There was something of youth about him, but his body looked as though it had been beaten by a hundred years of life. All thumbs and all feet, he seemed to move is ten directions at once. I expected him to fall flat on his face. I wondered how he found the energy to draw another breath. When he finally got through to me and I understood what he was saying, I was dumbfounded.

"Any church will do, even a church on one else will take. I've got to find something to do for God. I've got to find a chance to do something for people. You travel a lot. Maybe you will find a church somewhere." The words were so close to the old man's that I gave him the old man's address and said, "Who can tell. Maybe when two men pray for the same thing, they get the same answer."

I forgot about the whole event for a number of years and then one weekend I found myself back in the same city and decided to drive out to the little church and see if the old man was still there. I was surprised when I saw the little building. It had been repaired and painted. The inside had a simple beauty lost before in the dirty paint, cracked plaster, and scarred pews. All the years of neglect had been covered. You could still see where they were, but the attempted repentance made them an important part of the simple beauty.

A number of people greeted me warmly and several ask me to dinner. I hedged hoping to find the old man and be invited by him. Finally, I asked for him and they told me he had died. "He must have found you a great preacher," is said noting the changes. They smiled and said, "He found us the man the Lord wanted us to have. That is always the greatest preacher in the world."

In place of the self-concern I had noted before, I now felt something good and strong. There was a unity of purpose. "He must really be a great man," I thought, "to have brought about this change." I waited for the prelude to end so that I might see him.

The preacher came in and the people stood to sing. I had trouble finding my feet. This greater preacher, this man who had wrought a miracle with these people, was the man who was as close to nothing as anyone I had ever met.

I wondered at the changes God must have wrought. God hadn't done anything for his appearance. He looked ridiculous standing in the pulpit. In places his suit looked as it would fall of his body, in other places he was about to burst through. If the singing hadn't been so wonderfully distracting, I probably would have laughed.

"When he prays," I thought, "I'll have a chance to hear what God has done for his speaking. He must have given him the tongue of an angel and the wisdom of an apostle."

He didn't pray. A man from the congregation prayed. The deep rich voice poured forth not words but feelings of gratitude and praise for a wonderful, living, working God. I found my whole being praying with the man. It was thrilling the way he spoke the things I had longed to be able to say. The whole service moved in this way—up to the sermon.

The congregation waited, hushed, expectant as the minister moved ludicrously to the pulpit. He opened the Bible clumsily, took a long time finding his place. I waited. What a change the Lord must have wrought. My heart, so full, from the worshiping, waited. Then he spoke.

I could have cried. There weren't any changes at all. The raspy, stuttering voice vomited forth jumbled words in incoherent order. He still was the closest to nothing I had ever met. What caused the miracle?" I wondered.

I had dinner with the man who had prayed, "We're grateful you sent our minister to us," he said. "He's done so much for us. It's a shame the old couple couldn't have lived to see what has happened. We say it is the legacy he left us. He signed the contract for the year and then died. We were stuck with 'the man the Lord wanted us to have'. The Lord gave us His best. "His best?" the words came from my mouth so quickly that I was startled by them. "We had all kinds of *good preachers* and it always was the same thing. When we got this fellow, we realized we had to do something.

We began doing everything we could. We prayed, taught the Bible School Class, took over Mid-week Service, started calling. Some of the men began leading the singing and others began preaching on Sunday evening. We became aware of all that needed to be done and realized that even the most capable man couldn't do it all well. We learned another thing. We could do things better. In our prayers we spoke our feelings and they were the feelings of our neighbors. In lessons and sermons, we spoke of things that troubled us. We went to the Bible and found answers and also found that these same questions were troubling others. When we called on the sick we took time to help with the chores and the women folk cleaned up and cooked a good meal.

When we spoke of sin our neighbors knew we spoke from bitter experience.

The people began to realize that the church was important to the community. Soon we were fixing up the old building. Someone replanted the flowers the old woman had always cared for. The women began doing the cleaning she had so carefully done. Our past neglect bothered us, so we tried to heal up the scars of the past. They can still be seen but we are grateful for them. They remind us of the past and keep us from going back.

The congregation began to grow. One day our preacher came to us and offered his resignation. We didn't know why. We thought he had been offered a better church, so we gave him a raise and built a new parsonage. 'That isn't it,' he said. "You've grown and need a good minister." He was almost crying. One of the fellows said, 'You taught us to love God and to love men." Suddenly we all understood. God had given us His best. It doesn't take the voice of an angel or the wisdom of Solomon to teach the most important truths".

I've not been back for a long time, but every time I see a congregation advertising for a minister I think of the very fortunate congregation who got "the man the Lord wanted them to have," The Lord's man.

*First appeared Seek Jan. 7, 1990.*

# CROSS OF GOLD

There was obviously something bothering the young preacher. His usual confidence was gone. His voice was choked and strained. He stumbled over the words as he read the Scripture. His speech lacked its usual fluency.

The small rural congregation for which he preached held to the simplicity of worship of another era. The young preacher came to appreciate the sincerity of the people, and his confidence in God became somewhat contagious. Even though he was fresh from seminary, he stood before them with confidence and had spoken simply with conviction.

A cross of gold had been offered as a gift and was to be placed on the communion table. The young minister had questioned whether the gift should be accepted. Some of the people agreed that it would look out of place but felt it unwise to refuse a gift from the church's only wealthy member. He questioned but he hadn't made an issue of it. Quietly he tried to get the people to see the negative effect this gift might have upon the congregation.

The cross arrived and after some debate it was agreed that they would continue their practice of covering the communion table with a white cloth. It would be placed beneath the cloth, between the bread and the cup. When the covering was removed, there it would be. Everyone would suddenly behold the beautiful cross of gold.

On that first Lord's Day after the cross had arrived, there was a feeling of excitement, of expectancy, among the larger than usual congregation. When it came time for the Lord's Supper everyone strained forward as the elders removed the cloth and folded it carefully.

It was beautiful. The dull, battered communion set seemed drab and out of place next to it. The table was dominated by the cross.

No one noticed the pained look on the young preacher's face. "Isn't it beautiful," many had said to him following the service.

He answered, "Yes, too beautiful." No one seemed to catch the significance of his words. The cloth which usually was replaced after communion was left off following the service, so people could see the cross. Many paused for a final look as they left. Every Sunday morning it was the same. The people looked forward to the moment when their new treasure would be revealed.

So, it was on this Lord's Day, about a month after the cross had arrived. The young preacher decided it was time to take action. He was intently searching the faces of the congregation hoping for understanding of why people who desired to do right failed so often. His eyes sought out the elders, pondered each awhile and then went back to the bulge beneath the communion cloth. He wondered why such sincere men had accepted the gold cross when they knew it was not best.

Each man had his faults. He pondered these considering both the weakness and the man.

Short temper plagued one, bull headedness another. Cowardliness and thoughtlessness were among the many sins that were so obvious. He had been learning to work around their weaknesses; to be understanding of their faults, and they with him.

He looked at the women. With each as with the men he saw strength dissipated with weakness. Then he thought about the young children. There were always the young people; trusting, believing in the infallible goodness of the adults. What would happen to them if they should come to know the weakness of these men, or the women, or their minister before they knew themselves?

"How fortunate that we are not limited by ourselves," he had prayed that morning. Again, the people had not understood. Only a few wondered at these strange words.

Morning prayer, hymns, offering, announcements, Scripture reading, all passed quickly and with the passage of each his voice became more tense, his action less certain. When the elders came to the Communion Table, he seemed to collapse into his chair. Some thought it must be because their only wealthy member and benefactor had chosen this Sunday to attend and see his expensive gift. He never did much for the church, but his potential gave great weight to his words.

Jed and Seth were serving at the table on this Lord's Day morning. Jed had a quick temper but a short memory when wronged. Seth could seethe for months over some little slight or wrong. Both could and did make instant judgments and usually stuck to them. They liked the young minister but treated him as if he were a problem son to be kept in line with a firm hand until he had enough experience to be able to make more mature decisions. Both were exceptionally good men, devoted and sincere.

When they lifted the cloth, Jed turned red. Seth turned white. The congregation gasped. Jed shot a, *wait 'til I get you home,* glance to the preacher, and Seth looked at his feet. Most of the congregation tried to get an inconspicuous look at their wealthy member.

There on the communion table, in front of the bread and cup, in the center of the table, where the cross of gold should have been, stood a ghastly gallows, a perfect replica. The removing of the white cloth had set the noose swinging hypnotically. The few seconds of silence seemed forever. The preacher's hands were white as he grasped the arms of his chair. His eyes were averted like the eyes of a small boy caught in the act. There could be no doubt as to his guilt.

Seth's soft, calm voice saying, "Shall we pray," broke the silence. Jed had more difficulty with his voice during the prayer he offered for the cup. The Lord's Supper over, the choir sang a song that seemed to have no end. Then their young preacher began to speak.

"The cross of Christ was not a beautiful thing and was never meant to be beautiful. When it becomes beautiful it loses its meaning and power. This wooden gallows is to us, what the cross was to the soldiers, the Pharisees, and the crowd."

His voice was so tense people had to strain to understand what he was saying.

"One day Christ stood on a hill overlooking Jerusalem and made the decision between gold and wood. When He rejected the crown of gold, He accepted the cross of wood."

His voice began to relax as he continued the sermon. It took on its usual depth and conviction. "When we find it necessary to remake the cross, to cover its blood and shame with a covering of gold, to make it socially acceptable, we lose our right to exist as a church, as a people. It is only by helping people to see the cross as it really is that we can hope they will come to an understanding of God and His great love."

The people began to twist uneasily as he continued to talk of God's great sacrifice and the ugliness that made it possible. "We have allowed the cross to become a thing of beauty. So beautiful have we allowed it to become, we've not been able to see the sacrifice of Christ in the Lord's Supper. All we've been able to see these past few Sundays is a battered communion set and an expensive cross."

Some of the folk lowered their eyes in shame. The preacher's wife sat tall and gave her young husband a look that meant that it was all right. She didn't mind if they would have to move.

"There comes a time when the church has to stand upon a hill and look upon Jerusalem. There comes a time when she has to decide between gold and wood. This is the decision that is yours."

Jed was at the minister's elbow about the same time as the minister had reached the back of the church.

"That's the last sermon you'll be preaching here," he whispered into the preacher's ear as he started to storm out the door.

The rich man had come up about the same time.

"Jed, you mean that you're going to get rid of the first good preacher you've ever had. I've been coming off and on for years hoping to hear something worth coming back to. This is the first time I've gotten straight talk. It's the first I have seen the courage and conviction a Christian ought to have. You fellows keep too strong a hand on your preachers. I was counting on being able to come back and hear him again. I guess that's what I get for not doing my share around here."

The rich man's words carried a lot of weight in that church.

Jed got over his anger in a day or two. Seth was a year or so before he agreed with everyone else that they had the best minister in the county.

The rich man became the richest man in the whole countryside. He had swapped all his gold for wood and found it the best deal he had ever made.

Oh yes, if you should ever be visiting in a small country church and if when they uncover the communion table you see a small wooden gallows in the middle of the communion table, look around. The happiest man you see may be the rich man of this story.

*Published Standard 9-92, Just Between Us 6-13-93, The Helping Hand 2-25-97*

# LIVING WITH A PREACHER'S WIFE

It can be quite an experience living with a preacher's wife. Let me explain.

Last week, for instance, Betsy left the mayonnaise out on the kitchen counter. (Betsy, my wife, is a preacher's wife.) I thought it looked a little pale but then the cheap off brand stuff we buy often is a bit peaked.

It turned out to be uncolored finger paint she made for her class of two and three-year olds. Can you imagine a sandwich spread with finger paint?

The house abounds with such traps. When prowling late at night seeking something to eat, there is real danger. That chocolate pudding in the refrigerator just might be food for the pet worms being raised by her class. That unbaked cookie dough just might be play dough freshly made and ready for next Sunday morning. You won't mistake that stuff twice. Ugh!

The real winner was the Christmas cookies - rolled and cut sugar - a favorite of mine. It was fortunate I dropped it before I bit into it. The noise was deafening when it hit the floor. Luckily it did not hit my toe or anything breakable.

"Don. Don't eat my unbreakable Christmas cookies," Betsy called from the other room. As if I could accomplish such a feat. She must have heard the crash of it falling. "They're for my kids to frost on Sunday morning. It's a special recipe that won't break when they frost them."

"Great," I thought as I tried to imagine three-year-old Nathan trying to bite into it. That kid never gave up until he accomplished what he set out to do. I wondered if he would have any teeth left by the time Sunday school was over. I could just see him competing with his cousin Justin trying to devour one. I wondered if Betsy had a recipe for a cookie so sticky it would hold their jaws glued through church. It might even stick the seat of their pants to the pew.... Naw.... Even super glue's not that good.

There are other dangers when a preacher's wife runs a house. That cake or pie just setting there daring a knife to cut it asunder probably isn't for me. It has been prepared with great love and care for a hurting neighbor or a Ladies' Aid meeting. Death to whoever dares sample it.

"Home Sweet Home" under charge of a preacher's wife can take on an entirely new meaning. There is the possibility that I may arrive home tired from a difficult visit just in time to help put to bed a number of children we will care for until their mother is well. I may get to mop a muddy floor after the Bible Club Kids have used our dining room for a meeting place. It may be my lot to vacuum before the board meets. Or I may find my morning glories trampled where the kids from her Bible Club mysteriously changed into invading pirates racing across the deck of my porch and dropping from the end into the raging sea. My morning glories never could hold a candle to the beauty of kids having fun.

She's so busy I have to make an appointment to take her to dinner. She puts up with the mud I track in from the garden. (She met me at the door with a broom the day I spread the load of manure on the vegetable garden. Even her patience has limits. And has been known to put a stick of wood on the fire when I've been gone too long, and the fire is about out. Nothing is said about my once a month night out with my Christian writers group (all women but me).

She takes my phone calls, reminds me of appointments, cuts my hair and does half of my work.

Most amazing is the metamorphose that takes place when she changes from the stern teacher of many children and the wise 2ellor of hurting young wives into the beautiful, mature woman who welcomes me home and makes all the cares and problems disappear in the wonder of her love.

All told, I guess the dangers of eating some unknown substance masquerading as a delightful edible, are worth all the fringe benefits of living with a preacher's wife.

# WHAT I LEARNED WHILE IN THE HOSPITAL

*New Carlisle (Ohio) Sun*

**M**y recent trip the hospital to have my appendix out was a learning experience. I'd like to share with you some of the wisdom I gained in the hope it will help you be a blessing the next time you visit someone there.

## THINGS I LEARNED

1. If your operation left you stiff and sore, plan to be poked more that the Pillsbury Doughboy.

2. I soon realized that they never came to do anything for you unless you were asleep.

3. Each hospital day is 48 hours long; each night is 64 hours.

4. If you get rid of a bad roommate, you'll get a worse one.

5. Laughter may be the best medicine, but not when you have stitches.

6. They keep bed pans in the freezer and water in the oven.

7. An X-ray table is covered with ice before they tell you to lay bare butt on it and not move a muscle. You can't move a muscle. You are frozen stiff.

8. Before you get a CAT scan, they make you drink a gallon of Jim Jones Kool-Aid. They have it timed perfectly. Five minutes before the stuff goes through you, they stick you in an elongated donut and keep you there until your kidneys burst. That's how they know what's wrong with you.

9. The line on the IV is too short to let you into the bathroom.

10. The only thing I've found that is worse than eating from a bed tray while lying down is eating a picnic on a blanket spread over an ant hill.

11. All meals are served five minutes after they get cold.

12. They have a unique definition for food.

13.   Your bill pays the salary of an expensive dietician. It is her job to make sure you get a good meal with variety: red Jell-O, orange Jell-O, yellow Jell-O, and red Jell-O.

14.   If you are on a liquid diet, they will forget to bring you a straw.

15.   The phone always moves out of reach just before it rings and holds all calls until after you finally get to sleep.

# SOME OTHER THINGS I LEARNED

1. A hospital room is not a great place to entertain. Don't stay unless I am enjoying your visit. Pray, read Scripture and leave quickly unless I ask you to stay.   Check before you bring communion.  I may not be allowed such food.

2. Be considerate of the other patient in the room. Include him in the conversation if he is feeling well.  Offer to help him also.

3. Fruit is nice. If you've had an operation in the stomach area you will have to eat a lot of it.

4. Candy can be a big temptation especially if you are not allowed any.

5. A good book can be a joy. If it has to be returned, don't bring it.

6. I don't want to hear about people worse off than I. No matter how bad they are, I won't believe they are sicker than I.

7. Be positive, upbeat, encouraging, and helpful. Leave if I close my eyes to nap.

8. Good hospital etiquette is thoughtfulness and consideration. So is good Christianity.

# Theological

*This section I call theological. In reality, all I write is theological but I need a category for these articles. They may make you think a little more.*

*Published Christian Standard, 1977.*

# GREATER MIRACLES

For a long time, I was bothered by the words of Jesus, recorded in John 14:12. The verse clearly implies that the church is to do miracles surpassing anything done by Christ, and I found that hard to accept. Even the recorded miracles of the apostles didn't seem to surpass those of Christ. According to this passage they should have. Surely the apostles didn't lack for sufficient faith to fulfil this prophecy of Christ: and if they did lack faith to do what was promised, who now could supply the deficit?

Even a quick look at Christ's miracles leaves one with the question, "What can the church do for an encore?" Yet, I have discovered that the church is doing greater miracles every day and they have become so commonplace that we just don't recognize them.

**Look what Jesus did** - Consider for a moment the first miracle of our Lord (John 2:1-11) When he changed the water to wine, He performed a perfect miracle. It left nothing to be desired. The wine He created was not just good wine, but better wine. Now, how can we hope to improve on such a perfect miracle?

I am impressed with the way Jesus healed the sick. None were refused, none were left with partial healing, and none were told to wait for the healing to take place in time. When He commanded, a sick man took up his bed and walked. There was none of the excuses, delays, and failures so common today. What more could we hope to do for a sick man than Jesus did?

He gave sight to the blind, not just partial or incomplete sight, but perfect sight. To demonstrate this fact, one time Jesus asked a man what he saw. "Men walking as trees," the once blind man replied. Jesus touched him again and he saw perfectly. God wanted us to know that healings of blindness were not to bring some sight but perfect sight. How can Jesus expect the church today to do more for the blind than this?

He did many other miracles. He healed the lame, the deaf, and the lepers. He fed the five thousand, walked on water, and stilled the tempest. He did all this, and the Scripture still says we shall be enabled to do more. How can this be?

He raised Jairus' deceased daughter from her bed, the widow's son from his coffin, and the already decaying Lazarus from his tomb. As if this were not enough, He arose from the dead on the third day and ascended into Heaven forty days later. Yet the Scripture clearly says we are to do more than this.

**Greater miracles of the church** - the church does perform greater miracles as Jesus said she would. Every Lord's Day the church drinks from the cup of the Lord. The wine they drink is not wine at all but the blood of Christ; not literally as the Catholic Church teaches, not symbolically as the Protestant church teaches, but spiritually. In a very real spiritual sense, in a wonder of spirit, those who drink discerning the blood of Christ, drink literal wine but partake of the spiritual blood of Jesus. This miracle, changing wine to redeeming blood, surpasses the changing of water to wine.

We live in a very sick world. When the sick of this world hear the gospel preached by the church, if the hearing is mixed with faith, the sick are healed from their sin, and made whole through the redemption of Jesus Christ. The miraculous healing of a sin-sick soul far surpasses the healing of the physically sick body.

There are the spiritually lame, those who cannot walk with God. The church touches them with the healing power of the gospel, and they leap with far greater joy than any who threw away crutches.

When the spiritually deaf have their ears opened to the truth of the gospel and hear for the first time the words of hope that once had no meaning to them, it is a greater deed that has been done. Is it not a greater blessing to hear the word of the Lord than to hear the song of a bird?

Leprosy is a foul, disgusting disease. It slowly rots away the flesh until the whole body is corrupt. When Jesus reached out and touched a leper and the flesh was immediately - before everyone's eyes - made whole and firm, people could not help but believe. Yet, it is nothing compared to the healing of a person whose whole life is corrupted and stinking from the leprosy of sin. It is a wonder to behold a sin - corrupted person, washed and cleansed in the blood of Christ. Not a scar is left. The soul is made whole and cleansed by the power of the gospel. It is truly a great miracle the Lord has placed in our power to perform.

Even this is not the extent of the miracles that the church has power to perform in this day. We see those who are spiritually dead raised to new life through the waters of baptism. This miracle has become so commonplace to us that we fail to see the wonder of it. We seem to be unaware of the power of God who wrought it.

What is wrong with us? If someone raised the physically dead, we would flock to behold it. Which is the greater miracle, the raising the physically dead or the raising of the spiritually dead? It is a greater wonder to see a man who is hopelessly dead in his sin restored to new life. He died to sin and is buried with Christ in baptism that even as Christ rose from the grave to die no more, that man is raised to begin eternal life in Christ. This is a surpassing miracle.

**Which kind of miracle?** The Scripture says that Satan will be giving his workers power to duplicate the miracles of healing the sick, giving sight to the blind, raising the dead (Matthew 24:4-5; 24). Therefore, we are to beware of miracle workers until we know they are of God and not Satan. How can we tell? This is the purpose of the greater miracles the church is to perform.

The false teacher and miracle workers who serve Satan are limited to physical miracles. They cannot work miracles of spiritual healing for then they would be defeating their own purpose. They must mix the gospel with untruth so that it won't heal a sick soul. They must preach in such a way that blind eyes won't see, and deaf ears don't hear the whole gospel. They must make sure that some sin is left to eat away the soul.

Most of all they must make sure that sinners don't hear that they can be born anew if they will believe in and participate in Christ's death, burial and resurrection. A saving faith is a faith great enough to enable a believer to let go of this life and die with Christ. It is a faith that will enable him willingly to be buried with Christ. It is a faith that will enable him to trust God to raise him from this grave that he might live with Christ.

Those who serve Satan will come as close to the truth as is necessary to deceive you. You may be sure they will never come to the fullness of truth that will save you.

If anyone comes claiming to work miracles from God, test him. The test is simple. If he works these greater miracles, he must be of God. Ask him how a person becomes a new creature in Christ. If he is of God, he will say, "He must have a faith great enough to willingly share the death, burial and resurrection of Christ in immersion" (Romans 6:1-10). Those who are false teachers do not believe Christ came in the flesh. (This refers to His death, burial, and bodily resurrection, and also to our faith in this which must be expressed in our death, burial, and resurrection with Him - 1 John 4:1-5).

Let us watch and beware, for the day of His coming fast approaches and false teachers are trying to steal away even the elect. Test the spirits lest you also be stolen away. Seek to work these greater gifts of healing for they glorify God and are the only remaining proof that God is with you.

*Portions of this article first appeared as a letter to the editor of the Williamsport, Pa Sun-Gazette, then in several Christian publications and many other publications.*

# WHEN CHILDREN RAPE

Central Pennsylvania television stations carried the story of three thirteen-year-old boys accused of attempted rape of a classmate in the school darkroom. The incident raised questions as to how such an unthinkable thing could happen. The shocking fact that the three little boys were charged shook the complacent community.

In typical fashion, the school didn't look for the cause of the problem. In seeking to make sure such an incident didn't occur again the administration sought to set in place procedures to reduce the risk. They didn't address the school's part in the incident.

In science class the boys learned they were not created in the image of a holy God but were animals, an accident of nature. Is it any wonder they acted like brute beasts?

In social studies they learned it is wrong to pass judgement on the behavior of others and that they must accept everyone regardless of how he/she lives. Thus, they learned that all behavior is equally acceptable.

They were taught that all lifestyles are equally valid ways to live and they should feel free to choose the one that would give them the greatest pleasure. They were encouraged to demand the right to decide for themselves what is right for them and what is wrong. Is it any wonder they took for themselves the right to satisfy the pressure of their newly-developed sex drive in this destructive way?

In health class they learned that it is natural and healthy and good to release their sexual needs without the restraint of moral repression. In fact, they learned that moral repression is evil, destructive, the only remaining sin. Is it any wonder they felt it a permissible way to express these new and deep feelings?

If we continue to teach young people they are animals we ought to expect them to act like animals. If we continue to teach them that sexual morality is a matter of personal preference, we ought to expect them to live without restraint, that uniquely human quality that distinguishes us from animals.

It is time to recognize that we can't have it both ways. The failure to teach Christian values results in non-Christian behavior. We reap what we sow.

The three thirteen-year-old boys are the product of attitudes taught in our society and enforced in the public-school system. If we cannot have positive values taught in public school, we should expect negative behavior.

It is time to give parents an alternative to public education or to return traditional values to the public education system.

# GRANDMA GOES TO JAIL

On days like this I wondered why God put me at such a job. It was late afternoon. The bright spring sun struggled in vain to get through the windows that hadn't been washed in fifty years. One hundred years of cigar smoke hung in the unvented air. I caught an occasional whiff of spring air that crept up the decrepit, narrow staircase. My head hurt, and I was glad I could soon leave for home.

It was Monday, March 7, 1988. I had to complete all the news articles for three different weekly newspapers by quitting time the next day. Would the small Upstate New York towns generate enough news to fill the papers? It looked as if there would be huge empty spaces.

I checked the three piles in the middle of the decrepit boss - secretary desk. I sat on the boss side, not that it meant anything. I definitely was not the boss. The secretary's side was never occupied unless a publicity hound or small-town politician stopped by hoping to con me into doing a story.

In one pile there was enough information to finish five stories in the morning. Until people got back to me, the stories in the second pile could not be completed. Those in the third pile lacked information I needed so I reached for the phone. I wouldn't complete them by deadline without a miracle. Just as I touched the phone, it started to ring.

An excited woman on the other end began talking so rapidly that I couldn't keep up. Just what I need, I thought, as I grabbed a pencil and started jotting down the things she was shouting at me - "Lima, NY!" That is outside our circulation area, so I started to cut in and suggest she contact her local newspaper. She continued - "Grandmother being brought from jail will be at the court house for a hearing at 6:00." That caught my attention.

Without making any commitment I hung up. I didn't want to get involved with a grandmother who was being jailed because the eighteen-acre plot upon which she lived was littered with her belongings. Besides, the woman on the phone sounded crazy. I tried to convince myself that I didn't need another story this close to deadline.

In spite of my reluctance, I looked at the clock. If I left a little early I could make the hearing on time. Crazy, I thought. Why even consider it? It meant missing supper, working on my own time and at my own expense. This paper was not a big operation as you probably guessed when I had to use a pencil to take down the story.

I would not go. My wife felt abused if I was late for supper and the boss got mad if I called her to say I would be late. It was a ten-cent toll call.

I got out the Polaroid camera (the paper was not a modern operation), started down the stairs, told the boss I was going for a story, and slipped out before he could object. Something propelled me along to my car.

A small crowd was gathered around the steps to the court house. At once I spotted - no, heard--the woman who phoned. She was calling a well-dressed, over-fed man every non-profane derogatory word in the dictionary. She was accusing the town official of fattening himself up at a helpless woman's expense.

I talked with her and she introduced me to the three young ladies who lived with their mother and father in the old trailer they were trying to rebuild. (The father was in hiding to avoid arrest.) While taking their picture, along with their children who also lived in the battered building, I learned the town officials were trying to force them out onto the street. It appeared that an expensive housing development wanted to expand onto those eighteen acres.

Because Suekie (the name by which the grandmother was called) refused to comply with town demands (she felt she had the right to live as she could afford) a fine of $50.00 per day had been levied against her. At that rate it wouldn't be long before they could legally take her property

Suekie Rogers arrived in the sheriff's car.

The next day I wrote, "Suekie was brought from jail, hands cuffed, legs shackled. The timid woman who stepped from the car held her shackled hands for the crowd to see.

"'My God, I can't believe this is happening in America!'" someone in the crowd gasped.

"A hush fell as the gutsy woman hugged her weeping three-year-old grandchild." (*Avon Herald*, March 8, 1988)

I let all my other stories go the next day. I called, checked information, was given leads, smelled the stink of power and money, was threatened, but continued to probe for the truth.

Just at press time I took the story downstairs to the boss. I knew my only hope was that it would slip through.

The phone rang just as I returned to my office.

"Don, I can't run this story," my boss said. His friend, who had warned me about libel when I questioned about his part in the affair had called my boss.

I argued for the story but lost. It wouldn't be printed.

Just before quitting time, the boss called again. "Don, someone just ordered 250 copies of the paper for distribution in Lima." God had passed the ball to someone else to carry. The presses ran with the story for a touchdown.

Suekie Rogers was returned to jail and released a short time later. She remained in non-compliance with the law. I quit the job before I found out what happened to Suekie.

Several times I wrote her to find out what happened. I even stopped in to visit my replacement and encourage her to follow up the story. I never learned what happened to the grandmother who went to jail because she wouldn't be pushed around by those who thought they were entitled to special privilege.

I know now why God put me in that job. God puts us where He wants us and asks us to do what no one else is willing to do. He does care about defenseless grandmothers who are thrown in jail.

He needed a voice to His words:

"Woe to those who make unjust laws, to those who issue oppressive decrees, to deprive the poor of their rights and rob my oppressed people of justice, making widows their prey and robbing the fatherless. What will you do on the day of reckoning, when disaster comes from afar? To whom will you run for help? Where will you leave your riches? Nothing will remain but to cringe among the captives and fall among the slain." (Isaiah 10:1-4 NIV).

It was exciting to be that voice.

# BACK TO BASICS

If the Bible is inspired, the work of God, then we cannot improve on it. If we add so much as a single word to it, we pollute it. If we remove so much as a word, we weaken it.

It is time to call on this generation to return to the Scripture and recover what my generation let slip. The slipping away from the Biblical plan of salvation is a prime example.

Ezra 9:4 shows a proper attitude toward the Scripture. "Then everyone *who trembled* at the words of the God of Israel..." (emphasis mine). We no longer tremble when we open the holy word - no longer fear the fate of the prophet who let the word slip.

We are beginning to sound like those foolish people who think they can improve on what the Holy Spirit has written. They don't hesitate to attempt to make the word more understandable, more agreeable by using their own words in place of God's.

'Taking Jesus as your Savior' is not a better way of clearly pointing a person the way to eternal life. Jesus' words are the best. Jesus said that "I tell you the truth; no one can see the kingdom of God unless he is born again." (John 3:3) You cannot improve on that and there is no excuse for telling someone to take Jesus into their heart. It is a meaningless phrase that has whatever meaning we chose to give it. Being born again pinpoints what we are to seek to understand.

An understanding of what the Bible means by the new birth is important. It obviously is pointing us to a process similar to a physical birth. Rom. 10 tells us that the process begins with the preaching of the Word and that the Word is made alive by the Holy Spirit. This corresponds to conception in the birth process.

As the preaching of the Word continues to be heard and as the Holy Spirit continues to act upon it, wonderful changes begin to take place. First comes a growing awareness of sin.

"Woe to me! 'I cried.' I am ruined! For I am a man of unclean lips, and I live among a people of unclean lips, and my eyes have seen the King, the LORD Almighty." (Isaiah 6:5).

"We all, like sheep, have gone astray, each of us has turned to his own way; and the LORD has laid on him the iniquity of us all." (Isaiah 53:6).

"For all have sinned and fall short of the glory of God," (Romans 3:23).

While this is happening the other side of the Gospel is beginning to grow in our mind. We begin to grasp the truth that our own attempts at being good are futile. Our only hope is in Jesus' blood and His righteousness.

New birth takes place in the mind. Rom. 12:2 makes this clear: "Do not conform any longer to the pattern of this world but be transformed by the renewing of your mind. Then you will be able to test and approve what God's will is–his good, pleasing and perfect will." This renewing of the mind corresponds to the new birth and continues after the birth is complete even as the physical body continues to develop.

At this point the development of the new person makes an important change. Convinced of the enormity of his sin, he begins to confess his sins to God and to those who are teaching him the Gospel. He can bring himself to do this because he becomes confident that through Jesus' blood His sins are covered. Without such confession salvation is not possible and the growth within the womb of the church will not continue.

This ongoing process brings us beyond conception to repentance. That this is a part of the new birth is obvious from Peter's answer to the question, "What must we do to be saved".

He replied, "Repent and be baptized for the remission of sins and you will receive the gift of the Holy Spirit." This Biblical answer is far more explicit than taking Jesus into your heart.

My Gospels professor was also the Greek professor. He drew on the blackboard the two pictures seen in the Greek work "repentance". The two pictures he drew were doubled pointed arrows. The one had the arrows pointed outward - the other inward.

**Turning from sin**      **Turning against sin**

He then continued to lecture on the meaning of only the first picture, turning away from sin. I was not gifted in Greek but was gifted in spotting logical flaws. It took me many years to understand how both pictures fit into the Biblical concept of repentance.

Let me draw a word picture of what I call the backside of personality.

My oldest daughter is very loving and acceptant of troubled people. She is generous and freely gives encouragement and wisdom. My other daughter tends to be self-centered. She is demanding and unbending, expecting people to do what she demands.

Now turn their personalities over and look at the backside. The first had to struggle to be organized; to make reasonable demands of people. It was not her natural behavior. She often would over commit and let things pile up. She struggled to keep herself in control, on track.

The other daughter is task focused. A natural leader, she gets things done. She is self-disciplined and has little trouble denying herself for the welfare of the group. She is usually in control of any situation.

The greater the God given gift of positive personality, the greater the negative side of that personality. God loves balance.

This demonstrates one source of sin in our lives, the one pictured in the turning against. The qualities that make us special are balanced by the weaknesses that compliment them. These weaknesses are the areas of our greatest struggles with sin. They don't preclude that we will sin but show a propensity for a related sin. This kind of sin requires the repentance seen in the second picture. We must all our life build programs designed to shore up our weakness. We struggle against the weak side of our personality. We turn against our sin as the second set of arrows show.

The other kind of sin is learned. We make a conscious choice to follow an unacceptable behavioral pattern and develop dependence to it. It is possible to turn away from this form of sin.

When the hurt from this kind of sin becomes great it is possible to seek God's help to turn away from it. It is pictured in the first set of arrows.

Because we teach repentance only as a turning away from sin, people with compulsive behaviors despair of overcoming, and usually given up trying. They seldom can turn away from this aspect of their personality. They can, however; in God's grace, turn against it and keep it in control.

Some would argue that rebirth takes place at conception. Life does begin at that point. However, it is at the completion of the birth process that birth is considered as taking place. It is from this point that we count our birthdays. Baptism is our spiritual birthday. Romans 6 makes this very clear and there is no reason for us to compromise this Biblical fact.

The church is strengthened when we lose the 5,000 who come seeking bread for the stomach and reject the Bread of Life (John 6:66). Those who chose to make the Bible fit them rather than let it change them to fit the Word need to tremble before the mighty Word of the Lord.

*The following appeared in my column in the New Carlisle (Ohio) <u>Sun</u>.*

# ON HUMILITY

**I** attended a unity meeting between the church I attend and another very similar group. I am very big on seeking unity based upon trying to discern the intent of the Scripture rather than pretending we all believe the same truth. I don't think much of seeking unity at the expense of ignoring the truth.

During breakfast I chose to sit with a group of ministers from the other church. Since foot washing was a major difference I asked them why they practiced it.

"It is a most humbling experience," I was told, and they proceeded to explain how much it meant to them.

Meanwhile their coffee cups became empty, so I got up and brought a fresh pot. Filling their cups, I poured the drizzle that was left in mine. They continued to explain how foot washing was most useful in keeping them humble servants of Christ.

When their cups became empty I brought another pot of coffee, not filling their cups quite so full. There was some left for me. Though I served them three times, filling their cups, they never realized that it was I who washed their feet.

The practice they referred to came from an event which happened just before the death of Jesus. When the Disciples gathered to eat the Passover meal no servant was at the door to wash their feet. Someone should have been there to do it. It was Jesus who got a basin of water and washed their feet drying them with a towel around His waist. Peter, who was too proud to wash the Disciples feet, was indignant when the Lord began to wash his.

When Jesus finished, He asked them if they understood what He did for them explaining He set an example of how they were to treat one another. From that time, it became clear that Christians were to be humble servants, not ruling masters.

Foot washing can be an inspiring experience. It can be a powerful picture of a basic, often abused, Christian teaching. Obviously, it is not foot washing that Jesus wants. It is the humble spirit of one who serves.

We ought not to be like the man who was proud of his humility. While this is funny to think about, it is an unacceptable oxymoron that is too often the attitude among Christians. Some who don't understand humility; think meekness is pretending they are worthless people with no good thing to share. That is the height of arrogance.

Humility is knowing that God created you to be a person of value. It is giving Him the credit for the skills you have and the good that comes from the life you live. A humble man is fully aware of all that he is able to do well. However, he also recognizes that this ability does not make him superior to those not so blessed but is a gift from God.

It is a most difficult quality to cultivate because we have a tendency to take the credit for what we do or suggest that God cheated us and didn't give us any worthwhile qualities to share. Once, when I was bragging about how good I was, a friend told me that people, who have to tell how good they are, usually aren't. I needed that rebuke.

When we take credit for what we are, we also tend to grab the rewards. The God given gifts ought not to make us think we are better than others. Rather the gifts we have are to be shared. For the rule of God is, "Use the little you have well, and you will be given more. What you keep for your own pleasure you lose." The Scripture says it this way in Mark 4:25 "Whoever has will be given more; whoever does not have, even what he has will be taken from him." The NIV, (Grand Rapids, MI: Zondervan Publishing House) 1984.

There is a second rule: "Seek honor and you will lose out. Serve humbly and you will be honoured" The Scripture says it this way: Luke 14:10: "But when you are invited, take the lowest place, so that when your host comes, he will say to you, 'Friend, move up to a better place.' Then you will be honoured in the presence of all your fellow guests."

The NIV, (Grand Rapids, MI: Zondervan Publishing House) 1984.

This means that if you have intelligence or strength, great wealth or influence, talent or ability, they are given that you might be a blessing to those about you. If you are kind hearted and generous, patient and understanding, wise and loving, this is from God and is a credit to Him rather than you. It does not mean you have a greater chance of making it to heaven.

Humility is vital to the Christian life because failure to be so is to deny that it is God who made you. Such people Lord it over those they ought to serve. Others fail to recognize the worth of the life God created them to live and they never become the person of value God expected of them. That is sad.

Are you humble? Here is a simple test that will help you determine if you are.

1. Do you know what you do well?

2. Do you see this as a gift from God or think it is your own doing?

3. To what extend do you use these abilities to make life better for others?

4. What are your weaknesses?

Your answers should help you decide whether you need help in developing humility.

*First appeared as an editorial in Williamsport Sun-Gazette, March 27, 1993*

*Also appeared in the unpublished book, A Way Up Out a look at biblical poverty programs*

# HEALTH-SAFETY-WELFARE

**D**are we ask, do politicians believe the destitute are better off living on the street?  Dare we ask, do they really believe that this is better than living in the non-conforming housing of the Sisters of Mercy?  What has gone wrong in this once compassionate nation?

Like Israel, which once was a nation of dead bones because there was no justice in the land (Ez. 37:1-14), we are becoming a nation of dead bones, a nation without justice.

Justice is giving people the right and opportunity to make choices and allowing them to cope with the results of those choices. This is what God demands when he demands justice - an end to laws that rob the poor of the choice to work and laws that put a family on the street, taking from them the option to live in substandard housing.

The politician cries, "HEALTH, SAFETY, WELFARE!" three words reputed to be for the protection of the poor, which tend rather to protect the special privilege of the more fortunate.

Mrs. Rogers was returning from jail to the court house for a hearing. A small group gathered to support her. As she stepped from the sheriff's car, she held her shackled hands high for the crowd to see. The hush that settled over the crowd was broken by someone gasping, "My God! In America!"

Her crime, she was fighting for the right to provide the best home she could afford for her children and grandchildren.

Politicians say, "HEALTH, SAFETY, WELFARE! and another blighted building comes down, removing an eyesore, increasing property values. The poor are driven onto the street. The church remains silent about the injustice but open a shelter - until the politicians close it down. This is concern for their HEALTH, SAFETY, or WELFARE? Ask the homeless person.

"HEALTH, SAFETY, WELFARE" and another business closes because protecting the "HEALTH, SAFETY, WELFARE" of the employee destroyed the business and put him out of work. The church which remains silent about this injustice opens a soup kitchen. Ask an unemployed person how his "HEALTH, SAFETY, and WELFARE" was affected by this loving concern.

A young man didn't have money for the rent or milk for the baby. He took his box of tools and went about the community fixing people's cars in their driveway. He worked out in the snow and rain. His work was good and cheap, and he was paying his bills. In the state where he lived, he was breaking the law.

"HEALTH, SAFETY, and WELFARE" - a man gets a few dollars and tries to build a home for his family. The laws written to protect his "HEALTH, SAFETY, and WELFARE" forbid his building the kind of home he can afford. The church asks, "Well you don't really expect us to allow a home like that in our neighborhood?" A just law? Ask the family trapped in a slum apartment?

A father and son were thrown into jail. Their crime, they decided to build the son a home the old fashioned American way - hard work. They broke the law in their rural community which forbids them to build using the wood cut with their portable saw mill.

We pass laws protecting the snail darter which require an expensive environmental impact statement before land can be developed. Can justice return before we obtain equal protection for the poor? We need a law requiring an economic impact statement on all proposed legislation. It would protect the poor who are economic victims of our "compassion".

The Ezekiel passage tells how God gave the dead nation of Israel flesh to the bones and the spirit of life to the body once they restored justice to the nation.

He will do the same for this nation of dead bones when we return to the poor the right to stand on their own feet, when we restore to them the right to live according to their means, when we reaffirm the right of every person to work.

# ARE WE SAVED BY WATER?

## A study of 1 Peter 3:20-21

**P**roper use of the Scripture demands that we begin with the assumption that it does mean what it says since God is not the author of confusion. He always means what He says in the Bible unless there is excessive reason to believe otherwise. Cultural ambiguity, problems with translation, or obvious use of language not literal (symbolic, satirical, figures, etc.) sometimes effect the meaning. In most cases, God does literally mean what He says in His word.

If the literal meaning of the words fit with other passages, such an understanding must be accepted unless the language is obviously not literal. To treat a passage otherwise would suggest we do not believe in the literal interpretation of the Scripture.

1 Peter 3:20-21 is a difficult verse of Scripture because it refutes common doctrinal error. However, since it is Scripture, we must conclude it means what it says. The issue is not, are we saved by baptism, but, in what way does the water save us.

The passage reads, "Who disobeyed long ago when God waited patiently in the days of Noah while the ark was being built. In it only a few people, eight in all, were saved by water, and this water symbolizes baptism that now saves you also - not the removal of dirt from the body but the pledge of a good conscience toward God."

The common approach to the problems created by this verse is to say it obviously does not mean we are saved by baptism. Such an approach refutes the inspiration of the Bible. We can't have it both ways. If the Bible does not mean what it says, it is not inspired.

In dealing with 1 Peter 3:20-21 the first question we must ask, is do we find the concept of being "saved by water" elsewhere in the Bible? The best place to start is the event referred to in this passage.

Peter illustrates his point using the story of Noah and the flood which destroyed the earth (Genesis 6-10). He does this, so we can understand the relationship between the Genesis account and the salvation which comes to those who believe in Christ.

In the flood we see a prophetic picture of salvation. The components are all there. There are those who do not believe. There are a few believers - eight in all we are told - including the preacher of righteousness, Noah. There is the ark Noah built, a flood of water that comes up from the ground beneath and down from the skies above.

Peter's words are explicit. The water functioned to save these eight souls in the same way that the water in baptism functions today to save the believer. Before we tear this verse out of our Bible because it does not agree with popular doctrine, we need to understand how the water saved the believers in Noah's day.

First, we see that the water only saved those who believed. The believers were identified by their works of faith. They built a huge boat upon a mountainside and were obedient in every detail to the instructions God gave. They proved their faith in the promise of God and entered the ark before God closed the door.

The second aspect is the power of the same water that saved the believers. It destroyed the unbelievers. It is this function of water, the separating of believers from unbelievers that Peter is trying to explain to us. They perished in the same water that saved the eight believing souls. By drowning the unbelievers, it saved the believers from the corrupting effect of sinners.

We find water functioning as an agent of salvation in a second major event in the Old Testament. The children of Israel were in bondage to slavery even as we are in bondage to sin before our sins are washed away. God sent a deliver, Moses, who was "drawn from the water". The first of the ten miracles of the Exodus confirm this event is about salvation. Moses turned water to blood pointing ahead to the day when Christ's side was pierced, and water and blood came out. We see other signs among the miracles that we are looking ahead to Cavalry. There was darkness over the land and darkness at the crucifixion. The death of the first born of Egypt prophesied that the death of God's first born would deliver all who believed from death.

Even the ten miracles did not deliver the Children of Israel. They had to leave the land of bondage and travel by faith to a land they had never seen. On the way they had to pass through the waters of the Red Sea. 1 Corinthians 10:1-2 says, "For I do not want you to be ignorant of the fact, brothers, that our forefathers were all under the cloud and that they all passed through the sea. They were all baptized into Moses in the cloud and in the sea."

This passage means what it says. The Red Sea is a picture of baptism. The waters parted. The believers passed through the water. Overhead is the cloud which is water. They are immersed in the Red Sea.

We see water functioning in the same fashion as it did at the flood. Those who believed passed through the waters of baptism on dry ground. Pharaoh's army, the unbelievers, tried to pass through, and the dry ground turned to mud, trapping foot soldier and chariot alike. The same water which was the salvation of believers was the destruction of the unbelievers.

We see then that the water of baptism serves two functions, both of them for the salvation of believers. It destroys the unbelievers who would enter the church through baptism. It saves the believers by separating them from the unbelievers.

It is important to note that baptism is not a work as some contend. It is an act of grace that God performs on the believer who has the faith to enter the ark or cross the Red Sea.

We find this water and blood in unsuspecting places. It was present following the sin at Mount Sinai when the law was given. Moses came down from the mountain carrying the Ten Commandments. He found the people worshiping a golden calf they had made. In his anger he had the calf ground into fine powder and dumped the gold dust into water. The people had to drink the mixture to survive their sin.

Did you see the water and blood in this instance of salvation from sin? Stir the water with the ground gold. It will turn blood red.

This picture carries over to the New Testament. In His first miracle Jesus turned water into wine (blood) (John 2). Is it surprising that in His first miracle Jesus turns attention to the failure of the law to save? Would not those who understand He is the Messiah also understand the significance of water turned into wine?

In His first salvation message He said you must be born of water and spirit (John 3). Some say water is a metaphor for physical birth. If it is a metaphor, then spirit must also be a metaphor or John's grammar is atrocious. You just don't balance a metaphor and literal on the two sides of a conjunction. Good interpretation demands that you accept the word for what it means unless there is a compelling reason to give it other understanding. With each instance of water and blood at salvation, the compelling reason to reject the literal understanding of this verse is reduced.

Later the problem with the baptism of Apollo (Acts 18) helps us understand what Jesus was saying to Nicodemus - baptism in water was not enough. You must also be baptized in the Spirit. That is why Apollo's baptism which was according to the baptism of John the Baptist was not valid in the Christian era. It was of water but not of the Spirit.

John calls attention to the water and blood at the crucifixion (John 19:34). He obviously thought the water was important or he would not have recorded it. Belief in an inspired Bible requires us to believe that every recorded detail is important.

Consider what the Apostle John had to say about water and blood. 1 John 5:6-9 "This is the one who came by water and blood--Jesus Christ. He did not come by water only, but by water and blood. And it is the Spirit who testifies, because the Spirit is truth. For there are three that testify: The Spirit, the water, and the blood; and these three are in agreement."

In light of the other passages, we conclude that this also is a piece of the puzzle. The early church understood that water was only a part of the salvation process and that of itself it had no redeeming value.

According to John's understanding of salvation, there were three factors, the Spirit which quickened man's spirit (began the process of new birth), the water in which the old man was buried, and the blood which washed away the sin. In his thinking all three had a distinct place in the salvation process.

There are, no doubt, many other places where we find both water and blood at salvation. These are enough to conclude that Peter speaks a truth for God when he says that we are saved by water. It is obvious that he does not mean water only. The water of baptism destroys those who do not believe. For those who believe, it saves.

There is a valid danger to this concept. Some would use it to teach water regeneration. The water without faith in the blood and the life-giving Spirit has no saving value. It is an inoculation against the new birth. It is destructive.

# DOES IT MEAN IT?

There is a popular radio preacher who is always suggesting that the Bible doesn't mean what it says. He uses a number of phrases for this purpose.

"Let's look at this passage more carefully and see if it really means...."

"It obviously can't mean ...."

"What it is saying is...."

"Now if we look at the original language we see the true meaning...."

"An understanding of the culture of their day will help us understand that this passage really means...."

He is not one of those kooks who seem to get on the air by some unexplainable wonder. He is considered rock-solid, Bible-believing and true-to-the-Word. Yet with passage after passage that conflicts with his doctrine, he refuses to submit to the discipline of the Word of God. He consistently suggests it doesn't mean what it says.

I listened to his broadcast carefully, trying to understand how he gets a large following in spite of his abuse of the Scripture. I found he is very positive in his statements and sincere in what he says. His tone of voice is persuasive. His arguments are so complex and full of earthly reasoning I doubt even he understands them. But he does come across that he is the one who is always right.

This is a common method of dealing with Scriptural thorns in the flesh, those verses which don't agree with what we've always been taught. We also often dispose of some passages with complex reasoning, hoping to escape the conflict between our belief and the obvious meaning. Thus, we are not distressed by his practice.

Let me show you how this preacher uses this method to escape facing obvious truth.

If he came to a passage saying that one and one are two and it disagreed with his bank balance, he'd say:

"It is obvious that the bank is wrong. One plus one does <u>not</u> equal two.

"Now listen to me carefully. This is very important. I want you to see this.

"Let me show why it just isn't so. Anyone should be able to see that this cannot be the real meaning.

"The Bible makes it very clear that when two people marry, they become one, <u>not</u> two. You can see that. Two people when they marry make one person. That is a basic Biblical principle so one plus one equals <u>one</u>, not two. (voice raised, tempo increased.)

"Let me prove it to you another way. Suppose I take a cup of milk and add it to a cup of water. (Matter of fact tone of voice.) Do I have two cups of milk? No! (Intensity increases.) This is obvious. <u>One</u> cup of water and one cup of milk when added together do not make two cups of milk or two cups of water. Anyone can see this and so we establish a Biblical principle which is undeniable. One and one does not make <u>TWO</u>."

His listeners accept and repeat his conclusion. He obviously seems to believe it so they conclude he is right and they are not smart enough to understand. They accept and repeat his conclusion, never mind that they can't follow his reasoning.

They ignore his faulty argument. No matter that there are numerous Scriptures that refute his conclusions. He only needs to concisely state them, and his listeners accept them. If he has to prove that ten passages do not mean what they say in order to prove his point, never mind. His doctrine must be right, even at the cost of saying the Bible doesn't mean what it says.

When I hear someone say that a verse does not mean what it says, in my mind I see a little flag person jumping up and down waving two red flags, shouting, "Danger! Danger! Proceed cautiously."

These warnings result in my examining doctrines I once accepted. My number one rule is that only in rare instances does the Bible not mean what the words obviously say. Digging deeper, searching a little more diligently, seeking for what the author intended to say, we may find that what we once believed is wrong.

Proper interpretation demands we begin with the assumption that the Bible means what it says. Otherwise, we make God the author of confusion. If there is undisputed reason to believe otherwise, we are free to look for other understanding.

If knowing the culture gives insight to the meaning, if there is a problem with translation, if the language is obviously satirical or figurative, a metaphor or simile, if there is no way to reconcile it to other verses; only then should we set aside the literal understanding of the words.

For instance, when Jesus says He is the good shepherd, I need a cultural understanding of a Palestinian shepherd to have an accurate picture of this passage. The shepherds of our culture drive the sheep. The shepherd of Jesus' day led the sheep, calling them by name. However, there are passages which teach this truth, giving me this insight.

Because there is no exact English equivalent for the word translated <u>perfect</u>, we need to understand that it means "without imperfection". Because of our usage of the word, we wrongly conclude it means "without sin." Yet the Scriptural concept carries the idea of something that is full or complete.

Another word for which we have no exact equal is the one translated <u>hope</u>. We use it to denote some event that we want very much to happen. My son "hoped" I would buy him a new truck. No chance. It was wishful thinking. It was not hope because it was not based upon a dependable promise.

When the Bible speaks of our hope of salvation, it is an absolute fact. It is not something we wish to be true - it is as true as though it has already taken place. There is no doubt or question. It is yet it is to be. It is a fact of the present that will happen in the future.

When Jesus says He is the door, it is obvious that figurative language is used. He means that He is the entrance to eternal life - the only entrance. No intelligent reader would conclude that He is a slab of wood that swings on hinges and has a latch.

If the literal meaning of the words agrees with other passages, a literal understanding must be accepted. Otherwise we cannot claim to believe in the literal interpretation of the Scripture.

Red flags waving, caution me to examine other Scriptures to see if I have missed the clear meaning of the word of God. A careful study of related Scriptures will help determine if perhaps the obvious meaning was missed.

It is important to listen attentively to the person who argues that the passage does mean what it says. The probability is it does.

At times those who equally love the truth and love the Lord will disagree. Having a body of Scripture to defend their position, if they argue to win, they lose. If they listen to learn, they win, no matter the outcome of the discussion.

Three important things that can happen when I honestly consider an opposing view.

1. I can be confirmed in the correctness of what I believe.

2. I can learn a greater truth which allows me to see the Word more fully.

3. I can find myself wrong and escape the enslavement of a false belief.

Whenever any one of these happens, I win. However, whenever I fight to win an argument, I lose. Right or wrong, I lose because I don't have the spirit of truth that sets me free. The spirit of truth is not the absence of error, but the desire to correct our error.

Two persons who love themselves and who are confident of their superiority by virtue of the truth they hold, may disagree. Each has favorite verses to defend his position. In the debate, if Scripture is twisted to refute those used by opponents, neither is likely to come to the truth because they are moving away from it.

Two persons who love the Lord and love the truth may disagree. Each has a body of Scripture to defend. Comparing their understanding of these verses, they seek for a greater truth than either has, confident that in the mind of God these conflicting truths merge into a perfect unity. As they listen they move closer to the absolute truth, closer toward each other, confident there is a truth to be discovered. Though they may never agree, they are bound together as brothers and sisters by the greater truth both recognize exist but neither fully understands--<u>love</u>.

# GETTING OUT OF GOD'S WAY

**W**hen God sends our children through the fires to purge the dross, to purify them to His service, we often try to snatch them from the flames.  If we succeed, we destroy or weaken the work of God in their life.  The day I tried to snatch my son Joel from the furnace, I failed - Thank God.

I couldn't see it at the time, but my suffocating controlling love was driving my son, Joel, to jail.

I now understand. Attempting to free himself from my demanding love he rebelled. First smoking, and then drinking--on to staying out all night--drugs, he was determined to do it all, to force me to give him room to discover who he really was.

I reacted, tightening my grip, fearful of losing him.  In desperation he broke loose. Gone several days, he returned filthy, but not broken. Something, he never told me what, had scared him into coming home. My heart struggled to survive the fear I felt as I tried to understand what was happening to him.

My intense struggle with Joel also became one with God as He insisted He loved Joel. I knew He did--knew He loved Joel better than I-- knew that in my head. Yet the battle went on until the time came for me to give up, to let God have him. Making it a matter of faith, doing what I knew God was demanding, took a crushing blow.

See what I've done, my heart cried to the Lord as my son and I yelled at each other neither listening. We screamed because love still existed between us and it hurt. What we said was not love.

Later Joel and I were having a rare moment of talking rather than shouting. I was probing, seeking for a new hold that would enable me to regain control of him. He could see through what I was doing. No matter the cost, he was determined to be free.

Suddenly he cried, "I hate you." There was intensity, a reality to his cry that convinced me he meant it. I gasped, fought a pain that ripped my soul. The words cut because he had finally broken the bond of love and he was free.

I was still trapped in a love I could not control, a sick love that was slowly suffocating both of us. I wanted to hate him that I might also be free of the hurt.

I tried to hate but couldn't. He was my son. Then I understood that God's love was stronger than mine. He would never let go of me or Joel no matter how much we hurt Him. I gave Joel over to God.

"I love you." My shallow words seemed to drop to the floor unheard. I had not yet learned to give them honest meaning. Now, perhaps too late, I tried. "I'm sorry I've made of mess of things and don't know how to make it right. I never learned how to love as I ought. I understand your rejecting me as father. I am letting you free of me, so you can find God, a father who won't fail you as I have. From now on you will have to answer to Him, not me."

All this time Joel was yelling, "You can't do that. You are my father. You've got to take care of me."

I continued telling Joel, "We all have to account for what we do, and we can't escape by putting things over on Him. At times His love does hurt, but it is always wise and good. When we chose to please Him, He is free to bless us.

"You can't do that," he continued to scream. You can't disown me. I'm your son."

The words exploded in my head and I struggled to hold to the first really loving thing I had done for him in a long time. I was finding just how difficult quality love could be.

"I'm your son. You can't give me up." He cried with sobs one does not expect from an almost grown boy.

I tried to raise my arms to reach out to him, to hold him as I had when he was little. They were so heavy they fell back to my side. It was as if God were saying, "You've given him to me. He is my son now. You stay out."

When I turned to leave, he screamed one last time, "You can't do that! You <u>love</u> me."

I could do that. By God's grace I was finally learning to love, and it hurt more than any pain I had ever felt.

Two weeks later he was in jail. I never expected God to work so fast and certainly not so extremely. Joel had gotten drunk and tried to kill a friend.

I did go visit him as soon as I heard. They brought him into a room with a small glass window. He picked up the phone through which we were to talk. His head was down. He wouldn't look at me. He kept as far in the corner as the phone would allow. I struggled with a need to break through the glass that separated us and again take control of his life.

"You know why you are here don't you?" I asked quietly, not accusingly. He nodded. "You know why I can't bail you out?" He nodded, stealing a glance at me out of the corner of his eye. He expected a sermon. We both knew that he had to account to God. It was not my place to preach the usual sermon. Yet my old pattern of giving to him in a way that would meet my needs at his expense kept tempting me. But for the window between us, I could not have left him in God's love.

Two months later, Christmas Eve morning, all this ran through my mind as I prepared to leave for work. I struggled with the desire to interfere with God's work and bail Joel out. After all it was Christmas Eve.

My wife raised her eyebrows as I tried to convince her God wanted me to take charge again. She didn't say anything, but I knew what she was thinking--Here he goes again, controlling, manipulating. He needs to leave Joel in God's care.

"I'll leave it up to God," I said. "Tonight, when I close the shop, if I have the Five Hundred Dollars bail in my pocket, I'll go and get him out."

I caught the tightened lips and the slight shake of her head as Betsy saw through my "deal with God". After all it was Christmas Eve and there would be all those people coming to my shop for last minute gifts. It shouldn't be hard to end the day with Five Hundred Dollars.

In my junk shop, The Old Creamery, I had everything from authentic junk to fine glass; from bikes to over 100,000 used books, paperback to rare volumes. There were over a million items from colonial era to pop plastic. Everyone knew that if you didn't know where to get it, go to The Old Creamery.

Customers did come that Christmas Eve. They looked and poked. But shop lifters were the only ones who went away with my merchandise. I dropped prices, made offers no one could refuse, dug into untouched stores for unbelievable items. In desperation I fought to sell. No one could be tempted to defy God and buy.

It was time to close and all day I sold very little. There was no need to check the cash register total.

"I could write a check," I thought as I closed the door. I paused, waiting to see if God was testing me, my faith believing that one last customer, one big sale would happen just before I locked the door.

There wasn't a car on the road. Jail was the opposite direction of home. I locked the door and turned my car toward home.

The steps seemed unusually steep. I pushed against the kitchen door and entered. My wife was at the stove getting supper. One glance at my stooped shoulders and crestfallen face answered her unasked question. The phone rang as I leaned against the door to close it. I took the call.

"Dad, can you come and get me?" Joel asked.

On the way home from the jail I asked him how he had gotten out.

"I was praying, asking God to let me out. The judge called and told them to let me go," he said.

He looked quickly up at me, and then looked back down. I could tell he was expecting a sermon and that he already knew what it would be.

"I am glad," was all I said.

Surprised at my reply, he looked up and right into my eyes. He didn't realize that when I turned him over to the Lord, I first turned myself over to God more totally than ever before. I was struggling to love wisely.

Staring hard at the road, watching the snow dance in the lights of the car, I suddenly realized how close I came to taking control of his life. I almost destroyed the work of the grace of God taking place in him. If I had bailed him out, He would not have learned that God, not I, would get him through the tight spots. Because I kept out of it, he learned that God answers his prayers and is a far more dependable father than I.

We were going home for Christmas. He now trusted God as he once looked to me. By giving up what really belonged to God, I found what I wanted most, a healthy love.

It is true. Only what you lose to God do you save.

# YOU NEVER STAND ALONE

The porch swing was a pleasant place to think about what lay ahead; remember what lay behind. Across the road a trout stream bubbled contentedly. I gave up the hope of finding time to fish. Scanning the mist shrouded mountainside beyond the stream, I watched a deer hesitantly step from the shelter of the woods into the pasture to feed. There comes a time for us all to step from security into life.

A car went by, the first all evening. The book I had been reading clattered to the floor. Only the outward appearance of peace remained in my life. It was time to prepare for war.

"It was great, while it lasted," I prayed contemptuously. As quickly as the thoughts exploded in my mind, I imagined hearing God respond, "Ungrateful brat."

I sighed. "Forgive me, Lord. The peace and rest has been wonderful. It's OK with me to let it begin again."

I could see it coming again and didn't want to be involved. There was still remembrance of the hurt from the last time. Poor folk were going to be trampled and it looked like I'd be chosen to stand in the way again. As a Christian, stepping out of the way was not an option. This time I would try to be ready. Hopefully I would not be trampled as before.

When I came to Cogan House - it lays hidden back in the woods, off Route 15, north of Williamsport, PA - You turn at Fry's Turkey Ranch - the leaders of the church told me there wouldn't be opportunity for much growth. I would have plenty of free time to write.

About thirty showed up for my first sermon. People tend to show up for the first sermon. It was seventeen degrees below that morning. Glen said it was twenty-one below at his farm. I was instantly warm when I entered the badly in need of paint country church building. Bob Lowe took one look at me and said, "Well he can't be too bad if he can grow a beard like that."

I knew I belonged. God had called. He wanted me here. There were so many ways it had been confirmed. Before I was settled in, I would need the confidence of that confirmation.

I soon saw what the members of the small church could not. Back in the woods were expensive new homes. The largest development in the county was scheduled to begin in the back yard of the church.

The local people were debating <u>Flatlander</u> influx. (Flatlanders are those not born in the mountains.) They were unwelcome because they threatened the quiet existence that had resisted change over the years. It was easier to believe the intruders didn't exist.

I soon learned they were also debating the proposed county zoning. It was this disturbing news I pondered as I viewed the quiet countryside from my porch swing. While the township debated, the issue had been decided by the county. The only choice left to the people was whether they would zone themselves or be zoned by the county. Cogan House would be zoned.

Try as I would I couldn't regain a quiet spirit. I picked up the book I had been enjoying and put it on the shelf where it sets unread. There was work to do.

It was time to write a series of sermons on the Biblical principles that guide all successful poverty programs. If the congregation was to support me, there had to be a sound Biblical foundation under them.

My next goal was the creation of a community newspaper. I named it <u>Life in Cogan House.</u> I wrote about how the proposed zoning would affect each of them. The pen is still mightier that the wealthy.

Predominately rural Lycoming County, PA was faced with a difficult problem. The countryside was being ravaged. Old rusty trailers were being propped on the steep mountainsides to be used as hunting cabins. The working poor would buy a few acres of rather worthless ground and set an old single wide trailer on it. The wooded beauty along the country roads was suddenly broken by a small junk yard or a barn yard car repair shop with wrecked cars accumulating. There were tar paper shacks with the rusting hulls of abandoned cars scattered about the property. Rusting farm machinery of another era lined fence rows.

For the most part the countryside was quiet and untouched. The streams ran clear and springs trickled from hillsides. However, it was becoming obvious that change needed to be controlled. If you looked back into the trees, expensive homes could be seen sprouting up. Hunting clubs had bought up huge tracts of land. State game lands accounted for much of the land mass. People were crowding onto what little land remained.

To protect the countryside and to assure orderly development, the Lycoming County Planning Commission began to prepare a county zoning ordinance. They held area information meetings and kept the people informed of their intent. There was a refreshing openness on the part of Jerry Walls, executive director. He did not dodge the hard questions. They were answered with forthrightness.

However, there were members of the commission who were supporting an ordinance which would assure special protection for wealthy home owners. They did not expect the opposition they were to get on these regulations. At issue was the apartheid concept that communities have the right to protect their property values by excluding unwanted people. After all, no one wants a tar paper shack next to their One Hundred Thousand Dollar house, even if the shack was there first. Zoning is one of several methods used today to achieve this protection.

For ten years I fought bad zoning at a small upstate town that once had a healthy mix of prosperous and poor. At the edge of the village I ran <u>The Old Creamery Emporium and Book Shop</u>. A hodgepodge of clutter, it had a million different items including one hundred thousand books. You could buy anything from a used bike to a Weller pitcher - from a paperback romance novel to a vellum covered book from the sixteen-hundreds.

For some time, I didn't see what was happening in the town. Then many of my favorite customers began moving away. What I discovered was that laws were being passed which forced the poor out of the community. This became clear to me when a law was passed requiring a lot of five acres before a building permit would be issued. The cost of building in the town became prohibitive for all but the wealthy.

Since I wrote a column for the local paper entitled <u>Troubling Truths</u>, I began to expose what I discovered happening. This made me very unpopular with "The Boys Uptown", an unofficial ruling body. People would come to me quietly and give me the information I needed. Few would stand openly with me.

One day I received a list of six people who, I was told, were the targets of an "external appearance" law. I was told the law had been written with the intention of driving them from the community. I kept the list secret but attacked the law by showing how it would affect citizens. I made it clear that I would demand uniform enforcement. That meant that everyone with a tire swing in their yard would have to remove it.

Flowers planted in anything except flower pots would not be allowed.

The law was modified. The six never knew what almost happened to them. I was now in big trouble.

The change in the law was at most a partial victory, one of the few I won. I did succeed in getting the assessment of some outstanding homes doubled when I pointed out that the poorest homes were over assessed. High taxation of poverty homes is an effective way of forcing the poor out of the community.

Slowly it became clear to me that building codes, tax structures, and zoning regulations were driving the poor from the community. As I began to expose these methods, it became increasingly more difficult to get my column in the paper. The power of those whom I opposed slowly drove me back. In an effort to be less vulnerable, I sold my business. The Creamery wasn't "conducive to the atmosphere of ____ ." I had survived thus far only by the grace of God.

Then when it seemed there was no way left to speak out, the Lord opened the position of

news editor for three area papers. I had no
training, no experience. But I was where the Lord
wanted me, doing what the Lord wanted me to
do. That made all things possible.

The day I wrote the story about Suekie
Rogers, the grandmother who was put in jail
because she couldn't meet community standards
(in a neighboring community), the boss called up
to my office to say he couldn't print the story. A
little later he called up to say a woman just
ordered two hundred fifty copies of the paper.
He ran the article.

I was the only member of the news media to
cover Suekie's trial. The story read in part:

"Mrs. Rogers lives with her husband, three
daughters, and three grandchildren on an 18-acre
plot...The area had once been a dumping place...."

"Suekie was brought from jail, hands cuffed,
legs shackled. ...the timid woman stepped from
the car...held her shackled hands for the crowd to
see.

"'My God, I can't believe this is happening
in America!" someone in the crowd gasped.

"A hush fell as the gutsy woman hugged her weeping 3-year old grandchild." (<u>Herald</u> March 8, 1988)

My days were numbered. I had done all I could do. God moved me to Cogan House and a much needed rest.

Now it was happening again, and I wanted out.

It wasn't long before the day came when I had to stand alone at the planning commission meetings and defend the rights of the poor. The odds were against me, but this time I had people praying for me. While I supported zoning, I stood firm demanding it not be used to create homelessness.

I was losing the most important battle, the one to preserve the rights of people to live in single wide mobile homes. One member of the planning commission suggested that if they couldn't afford homes they could live in town houses, "which are cheaper than trailers." I thought of the French Queen who said, "If they don't have bread, let them eat cake."

The planning commission felt that restricting single wide trailers to ghetto parks would curtail and contain the abuses that are common to separate lot trailers. Since they are affordable housing, they tend to attract a higher ratio of indolent home owners. The result is an increase in homes that are not properly maintained. The result is a demonstrable reduction in the value of neighboring homes.

This issue was well summarized in a planning commission memo dated Sept. 13, 1991.

"Many residents of these rural Townships questioned the prohibition of single-wide mobile homes. These are seen as the primary low-cost housing alternative which is needed for young people just starting out, until they can afford a conventional single-family home, and the elderly who want to live near their children but still have privacy. On the other hand, concern was also expressed about the possible impact of mobile homes to the property values of existing residential areas, particularly by residents of Muncy Township. Some residents expressed the opinion that single-wide's, should be permitted with special controls."

Another memo showed that the single-family housing composition of single-wide mobile homes in some of the townships was as high as 36.4% with the majority having 20% or more. This fact, uncovered by chief planner, Kevin McJunkin, was a surprise to most.

On Oct. 5, 1991 the Williamsport Sun-Gazette printed the following letter from me.

"Ideal zoning protects the right of the rich and poor to live together according to their means. It assures the equal right of both to live within the community, and it seeks to maintain an economic balance within the community. Where this is achieved, a healthy social community is preserved, and a sound economy is assured.

Ideals are never reached by mere mortal man. However, they give us lofty goals that carry us to heights we would never reach if we had no dreams to lift us.

The Lycoming County Planning Commission has been working hard to achieve a zoning plan that will preserve the social health of the county. They have accomplished a remarkably compassionate ordinance. Their work has been a thankless task. It does have a weakness.

There is a phrase often heard at their meetings. It would seem that some of the members are seeking to 'preserve the natural beauty of our county.' This is commendable. However, it is not possible to legislate beauty. To some, an old single wide trailer perched precariously on the mountainside is ugly. They see the bikes strewn about the yard, overgrown grass and the overflow from the small home that litters the yard.

I see this same trailer, but I see a single mother, a gutsy woman struggling to give her two children a chance in life. I see her desperation as she seeks to eke out an existence on a minimum wage job. I see the trailer and I see something of eternal beauty. A zoning law that does not allow this woman the right to live according to her values and ability is not a good law. We can't legislate beauty."

At one meeting of the planning commission, I made an appeal for an ordinance that would seek to insure economic diversity in the county.

Pointing out that while Cogan House had many poor it had little poverty because people were relatively free in the township to live according to their means. I also noted that social and economic health was possible only where diversity was protected by law. If zoning were allowed to drive the poor from other areas of the county to Cogan House, the township would be overwhelmed in their efforts to support those in need.

In a confrontation with Jerry Walls over these issues I concluded that "Life is not always beautiful," suggesting that members of the commission obsessed with preserving "the natural beauty of the country" were in effect creating an ugly repression of the rights of the poor.

The opposition to single wide trailers melted. The planning commission did add regulations increasing set up costs, increasing the chance that some people would have no option but to live on the street. When I opposed the regulations as unnecessary and repressive, they used the three magic words that consistently rob the poor of their right to live as they can afford - HEALTH, SAFETY, and WELFARE.

While I made the commission back off from many of its repressive goals, it wasn't over. There are members of the planning commission who will slowly whittle away at the justice won for the poor. There are some people in Cogan House who will never come to the Christian Church because we ruined their dream of a community where only their kind could afford to live.

I did learn this. Those who stand alone are not alone. They stand in the midst of a heavenly host. As long as there is someone to speak up against injustice, evil will not triumphant.

*First Appeared BUILDER Sept. 1994*

# PROBLEM SOLVING

Every church has problems. This is as it should be for only a dead church is without them.

Since new problems seem to develop faster than we solve the old ones it is important church leaders develop the skills needed to overcome them. Effective problem solving makes great churches.

I worked as a press person on a web newspaper press and when a problem developed, the boss would say, "I don't care how you do it, but solve it." The paper had to get out. There was no running from difficulties. Facing them was good training for when I became active in church leadership. I found the problem-solving skills I developed on the press also worked in the church.

After I left for another job, when problems developed they called me in to solve them. As a trouble shooter, it was up to me to find out why the press wasn't running correctly.

Everyone was standing around anxiously awaiting my arrival, looking at the clock, wondering how late they would be getting the paper off the press. The first thing I asked when I arrived was, "What is wrong; what is the problem?" If they said that the paper wouldn't go through the folder, I told them that isn't the cause. It is the effect caused by a problem. Because they hadn't learned to focus on the real difficulty, it was necessary to call me.

## FIRST STEP IN PROBLEM SOLVING

Churches need trouble shooters. They need people who are good at making things run effectively.

Solving problems in churches begins with identifying then. Like the press crew we often confuse the results of a problem with the real cause. When this happens all our energy is consumed trying to correct effects. Until the cause is addressed, anything we do will be temporary and need doing over and over.

Temporary solutions are sometimes the answer. I have used some ingenious makeshift methods for getting around the press problems. Fish line, dish soap, and the always valuable - gum have enabled me to meet the deadline. Then, when there was more time, get to the real cause, and a permanent fix. To continue for any length of time without identifying the difficulty can be disastrous because problems pile up until you are buried in sludge that overwhelms you.

Let me show you some examples of trying to correct the effects rather than the problem.

To increase attendance a church decides to have a calling night. This may work if the problem is that people have not been invited to church. However, if visitors come and are warmly welcomed and then ignored all week, chances are they will soon quit coming. If newcomers make three close friends within six months, chances are they will remain active in the church. If this is not happening, it is a problem that needs to be fixed.

If then the problem is that members do not open their social circle to seekers, a calling program will not solve the attendance problem. Small dinners or get-togethers which include new people may be the solution. Small groups within the church may be a second. Until the members open their social circles, whatever is done to solve the low attendance will be a temporary patch.

A second possible cause of empty pews may be a failure to understand that effective evangelism starts with meeting the needs of people. If the congregation begins need meeting programs, and the minister preaches practical, need meeting sermons rather than abstract doctrine, or simplistic answers to people's problems, the pews will soon begin to fill.

If the effect is empty pews, the first step is to discover why they are empty. A preacher was lamenting the fact that many did not come to the Sunday school class he taught. I remarked that if the food was good, the people came to eat.

## TRY EASY SOLUTIONS FIRST

Back to my press, I usually watch while the recalcitrant press runs. After a while I will make a few adjustments to see the effect on how it runs. I ask questions of the press person. What has been tried? How did that work? When did the problem develop? What changes were made before the problem developed?

I list the possible causes, first checking out the easiest or the most likely solution. When I identify the real problem, the hardest part is over.

One time the problem was failure by the press person to follow the procedure I had set. I recommended a return to procedure and everything went smoothly. I had one press person who constantly departed from procedure. I got mad.

"Dan," I said, "it is not very smart to do things your own way. If you are wrong and mess things up, you're in trouble for not doing what you were told. If you are right and show me up in front of the boss, you are really in trouble."

He didn't get the point and continued to do things his own way. I had to point to him as the problem.

## WORKABLE SOLUTIONS

Once the problem is identified and I consider the possible solutions, trying the simplest or most likely first. I then move on to the more complex until a workable solution is found. Too often churches tend to try the most complex solutions first.

A minister wanted to begin a substance abuse ministry. He was certain that it would solve the empty pew syndrome. No one in the congregation had any experience in this area. Relying upon my press experience, I suggested that the member's first record needs within their experience. Once busy helping with things they understood, the church could reach out to meet more difficult needs. When they have recovering alcoholics capable of leading a substance abuse program it will be possible. Meanwhile, because the church identified a problem simple enough to handle, they will be able to go on to greater things.  The Scripture says that if we are faithful in simple things we will find grace to go on to greater.

Mothers of grown children started a Mother's Morning Out.  Some of them baby sat pre-school children while the young mothers enjoyed a reprieve with an experienced mother who shared wisdom and offered a sympathetic ear.

## THE VITAL INGREDIENT

Perhaps I have over simplified this whole concept.  Identifying a problem and then finding a workable solution usually isn't simple.  Daniel, who worked on the press, was of a religion that didn't believe God has a part in our everyday lives.  We were having one of those days.  I couldn't find the cause of the problem and the waste paper was knee deep.

"Daniel, do you think the Lord can run a press?" I asked.

"He can but He won't," Daniel answered.

"He had better." I replied. "I can't find out what's wrong."

As I prayed my hand brushed a loose bolt. I tightened it up and the press ran smoothly. Daniel didn't have much to say the rest of the day. As the press purred contentedly he did do a lot of muttering - something about God not being about to run a press.

If God can run a printing press He can run a church. I suppose one of the biggest problems churches face is people who won't give God a chance to run things.

I tried out for a church once. They asked me if I could solve their problems. I replied that all I could do was help them discover what God would enable them to do. I didn't get the position which is why I fixed stubborn presses.

God must be a central figure in all problems solving whether it be in the church, the home or on your job. However, God chooses to work through His people.

Most churches have someone who works at a job that demands problem solving. This person is one of your most valuable assets. Make use of this resource. Applying the skills he uses on the job, can help identify your problems. You may learn that you don't need more Bible School rooms - you only need to use them more effectively. You may learn that you don't need a new minister - the one you have may only need to be free to use the special gifts God has given him. Let someone else do the things that the minister doesn't get done or doesn't do to satisfy you. The major preacher problem is not incompetent preachers. It is churches who expect a leader to be good at everything.

## PROBLEM SOLVING TAKES TEAM WORK

The answer is always there waiting for us to seek it. God takes great delight in hiding it in the most unlikely persons.

I heard of a truck which was stuck under a bridge. The driver had ignored the clearance warning sign and had slammed under, entrapping the truck. Huge wreckers tried to pull it out. They failed. Men pooled their knowledge. Yet it remained stuck. They were getting out torches to cut the truck free when a small boy asked, "Why don't you let the air out of the tires?" It worked.

When the press was impossible to control, I listened to everyone who worked on it. Sometimes the college student who tended the folder would say something that would give me the clue I needed. Sometimes it was the helper. Once it was the quiet little lady who ran the addressing machine. She was able to describe a strange noise she had never heard the press make before. People succeed who are willing to listen.

Often, we overlook the most important sources of knowledge. Those who are supposed to know, those who have experience usually are the ones with the answers. Yet many times it is the child standing by watching the tow truck who sees most clearly.

There is a tendency to overlook the elderly even though they speak from years of experience. How long has it been since you bent down to listen to a child? Have you ever heard words of wisdom from the retarded?

Chauncy came to church from the group home for the retarded. He wore a helmet because he might have a seizure. During the stilted services, his booming voice on occasion would call out "Amen". When the old hymns were sung, he never missed a note. The people were patiently tolerant of him.

When I welcomed him, his huge black hand swallowed mine. I was usually in too much a hurry to wait while he struggled to get a few words out. He didn't seem offended when I rushed off.

Then one day I discovered that the words he spoke did not come from his mind which didn't function very well. They were pulled from deep within his soul and they were pure gold, a rich treasure. Always he spoke to my need. I am sure he was able to see me more clearly than I saw myself. Yet he loved me and expressed gentle care for me.

Every member of the congregation is a part of the problem-solving team. Each is carefully selected by God and plays a vital part in the health and soundness of the group, not one member is not needed for the success in the mission of the church.

# GOOD SOURCE MATERIAL

The book of Proverbs was written to teach wisdom, insight understanding and discernment. These are the major tools of problem solving.

"How did you see what was wrong?"

"I don't know. I just saw it." This is insight.

"Why did you do that?"

"I don't know. I just knew it was the right thing to try." This is discernment.

"Who taught you that?"

"I don't know. I just know it." This is wisdom. All three are gifts from God given to enable us to solve problems.

"How did you know to do that?"

"An old man taught me."


# THE SIMPLE STEPS

The simple steps to solving problems are these.

1. Recognize that you have a problem.

2. Identify the problem making sure that you are not confusing it with the effect.

3. Try the possible solutions beginning with the simplest or most likely. Simple solutions are usually the best.

4. Develop the problem-solving gifts God will freely give.

5. Look for the answer you are seeking in the people surrounding you.

Read the book of Proverbs regularly. It is still the number one text on problem-solving.

Remember. Churches which become good at problem solving will be entrusted with even greater problems to solve. This is what makes a great church.

# POETRY

*I've actually been paid for some of my poems. That is an accomplishment in this day and age when poetry is not widely read. I've included a few because they say things I feel need to be said.*

*First published Devozing Jan/Feb 2001.*

# DESTROYING THE POWER OF HATE

I stood there on the mountainside

Listening to the voice of God.

You can't be serious, I thought.

Love my enemies?

Turn my other cheek?

Give to those who take?

Walk a second mile?

What kind of world would that make?

# A TIME FOR MIRACLES

Father, it is the time of year for miracles.

We want to believe.

Help our unbelief.


We know it is possible,

A virgin born babe in a manger-

It would be a little thing for such a great God,

Powerful, almighty God.


And it would be so much like You

Confounding

The intellectual

The mighty

The powerful

The proud

With a babe, new born,

Joy to His mother,

Without earthly father.

And all the old ways tumbling at His feet.


Father, it is the time of year for miracles.

We want to believe.

Help our unbelief.


We want to see good things happen-

The homeless warm

The hungry feed

War turned to peace

Violence smothered in love.


We've seen the power of your love.

The oppressed defended

The fearful emboldened

The rejected accepted

The down trodden raised up

The lonely befriended

The weak strengthened.


We have need of these miracles among us.

Make us the instrument of your love.

Give us wealth


A wealth of strength

To lift up the fallen

A wealth of time

To share with the lonely


A wealth of humility

To feel at one with the rejected

A wealth of faith that the sick might be restored.

Make us an instrument of your grace

That we might share our abundance

With a neighbor


That world peace might begin

In our home

That a neglected child

Might be comforted in our arms.


Father, it is the time of year for miracles

We want to believe.

Help our unbelief.

*First appeared: The Lutheran Digest Winter 1992.*

# GOD IS REAL

God is real,

as love is real.


I suppose that people

who have never been loved

doubt the reality of love.


Let me love you.

Then you will know

that God is real.

# THEY DID NOT KNOW
# THE CHRIST

They couldn't see the Son of God

a babe lying in a manger-

Neither Mary nor Joseph could see.


The shepherds wondered

but didn't understand.

The king saw a rival

and dared to kill.

The people, from all over the kingdom

wondered,

went home,

and forgot.


Until the king killed

all the boy children under two

and then, while the pain remained

they wondered.

Had they seen the Son of God

seen His wonder

His glory

His might?


In a manger?

A peasant mother?

A questionable birth?

It is hard to see truth

in its proper surroundings.


So today we can't see the Son of God,

because He isn't what we want Him to be.


We would have Him stop the war.

He would have us end our greed.

We would have Him feed the hungry.

He would have us share our food.

We would have Him comfort the lonely.

He would have us embrace the unlovely.

We would have Him stop the murder, the rape.

He would have us love the hurting.


We can't see God,

because He isn't what we want Him to be.

# TRAPPED IN OUR BODIES

We are so trapped in bodies that torment us.

Oh, wretched man that I am -

Who shall deliver me?

*First appeared: Jeans Journal Dec. 1987.*

# SUMMER LASTS FOREVER

Summer lasts forever when you're young.

When you have an eternity of golden days lying ahead.

How does it happen that they pass swiftly?

When the eternity is almost gone

and winter's cold is a thing to dread.

*Cleaning Toilets*

*Poetry Book 2014.*

# CLEANING TOILETS

Bitter bone chilling cold.
An old man slowly forcing a path
shovel full by shovel full
clearing a path so worshipers
feel a warm welcome.

A young man, watching, wondering why?
Pausing, wiping non-existent sweat from his aged
brow, young man, don't you know what Jesus
said?
He who is faithful in shoveling snow will be
considered worthy of cleaning toilets.
Is that not the way to greatness?

# About the Author

My first sale of an article was 1953. Over the years of a very eclectic career I published everything from a pre-school book to the book, <u>Teaching the Bible with Games</u>. Two of the three articles that appeared in Guideposts were chosen to appear in their anthology <u>Treasury of Hope</u>.

In addition to the Guideposts Christian Writer's Award (1974) I took first place in St. David's Article Contest (1990). Among the several writer's workshops I've taught was the North American Christian Convention (1989). My writings have appeared in over thirty periodicals, both Christian and secular. My poetry has sold many times.

My career in journalism included a column *Troubling Truths* which appeared in a number of newspapers over the years. As news editor for Sander's Publications (Geneseo, NY) I had the exciting experience of running down the stairs shouting "Stop the press. I have the story". I heard the press start up just as I broke the story that may have prevented a major ecological disaster.

Now over eighty I continue to write, reselling the many articles that still have relevance today.

**Author Don Fay:** It's almost sixty-five years since his first article appeared and his writing is still affecting readers. Add to that the fact that Don Fay had seven kids and still found time to write over one hundred articles, books, and poems and be published in a multitude of magazines. The diversity of his writing is also outstanding spanning the preschool audience to the Bible scholar. The readership varied from a few thousand to the five million readers of <u>Guideposts</u>. When Ann Landers reprinted one of his newspaper columns his readership passed seventeen million, at that time almost the greatest readership in the English language. He says he was able to accomplish this in spite of a learning disability partially overcome when he taught himself to read in fourth grade. He believes that it is God who enables him to do what is impossible for him to do.

34593767R00115

Made in the USA
Middletown, DE
01 February 2019